OFFCUTS:
Stories from The Shed

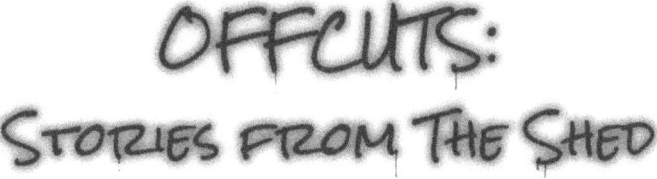

ST JOHN'S OXLEY COMMUNITY MEN'S SHED

Dave Shearer
Jim Pascoe
Bill Thirkill
Michael Reynolds
Trevor Armstrong
John Brown
Bill Barker
James Vernon
Darryl Dymock

Offcuts: Stories from the Shed

St John's Oxley Community Men's Shed

© Individual contributors 2021

Published by Armour Books
P. O. Box 492, Corinda QLD 4075

Cover Image: iStock: kaisersosa67 | Man opening doors of agricultural shed

Interior Design and Typeset by Beckon Creative

ISBN: 978-1-925380-378

A catalogue record for this book is available from the National Library of Australia

All rights reserved. No part of this publication may be reproduced, stored in, or introduced into a retrieval system, or transmitted, in any form, or by any means (electronic, mechanical, photocopying, recording or otherwise) without the prior written permission of the publisher.

Note: Australian spelling and grammar conventions are used throughout this book.

Introduction

THIS IS NO ORDINARY collection of stories. It draws on the varied experiences of nine men who have led very different lives, but whose paths have eventually crossed at Oxley Men's Shed.

In this book these mostly first-time writers have taken the opportunity to share some of their fascinating stories from the past with their families and with the wider community. Many of these are never-before-told tales, entertaining anecdotes that not only illuminate the writers' earlier lives, but often trigger our own memories too.

In these stories we meet a former fitter and turner who as a boy decided to see what would happen when he packed gunpowder from leftover fireworks into a fruit tin and lit the fuse; a retired meat inspector who had to escape hand over hand down a rope off a high church roof when his ladder collapsed; an ex-plumber who starred in a Bollywood movie and dodged bombs and bullets while driving a tour bus in the Middle East; a former photographer who once had the ultimate hand in a boarding house poker game; and a retired insurance underwriter who relives his late-night dash home to dive under the bedclothes before the resident ghost appeared.

Then there's a Vietnamese veteran driving an Army forklift who literally backed himself into an embarrassing corner with his commanding officer; an ex-teacher who was driving his prized first car through South Brisbane when the back seat caught fire; a former electrician who turned jackaroo to help out his mate on a cattle drive in northern NSW; and a retired agronomist who as a young man led a hiking group down a mountain during a cyclone, with intriguing romantic results.

This is a heady mix of yarns from a group of writers keen to tell their often remarkable, sometimes humorous, occasionally hair-raising but always heartfelt stories.

A message from the President, *St John's Oxley Community Men's Shed*

When the writing group started at Oxley Men's Shed in early 2021, I thought it was a good idea but I wasn't sure how it would go. We all have stories, but writing them down isn't everyone's cup of tea. Then they started adding to their numbers in the room above the Shed where they meet each fortnight. Within a very short time they were sharing their stories with the rest of us at our Tuesday meetings. We enjoy hearing those yarns, so it's great that these writers have been able to collect some of them in this book. For most of them, it's the first time they've recorded their personal memories in this way, which is good not only for them but also means they can share their earlier lives with their families. What's more, these stories confirm what we already know: we're a diverse bunch of blokes from different backgrounds, with different experiences and different skills. But the Shed brings us together.

— Martin Rankine

A message from the Parish Priest, *Anglican Parish of Sherwood*

I'm very pleased to see this collection of stories from the writer's group at St John's Oxley Community Men's Shed. In my work, I often come across bereaved families who know very little about the lives of loved ones who have died, and when the family do hear their story it shares another insight into these amazing lives. So, it's great that these writers are passing on their memories to other generations. The Shed has an important role in this community in helping older men maintain active minds and bodies, meet up with friends and share their skills. And the stories in this book remind us that we all have a need to be connected to others around us, across the street, across our communities and across the world, as well as to those we love and who love us. May God's blessing be on you all.

— **Rev Morris Rangiwai**

Contents

Introduction	v
A message from the president, *St John's Oxley Community Men's Shed*	vi
A message from the Parish Priest, *Anglican Parish of Sherwood*	vii
Dave Shearer	1
CHANDLERS HILL ROAD	1
HARRY SHEARER'S GENERAL STORE	3
DARLINGTON	5
SECONDARY SCHOOL	6
JOINING THE ARMY	8
Jim Pascoe	11
A CHANGE OF LIFESTYLE	11
LOVE IS IN THE AIR	14
A DROVING TRIP	18
Bill Thirkill	23
INDIA 1964	23
AFGHANISTAN 1964	26
ISRAEL 1966/67	28
ATLANTIC STORM 1967	31
Michael Reynolds	35
MAJESTIC THEATRE	35
THE SWIMMING HOLE	37

THE BOY FROM ROSEWOOD 38

POSTSCRIPT 39

Trevor Ross Armstrong 41

FROM MILK RUNNER TO WEEDS RESEARCH
AGRONOMIST 41

A.F.R.S. ADVANCING INTEGRATED WEEDS
MANAGEMENT 49

VENTURING UP AND DOWN MOUNT BARNEY 52

John Brown 55

MIDDLE RIDGE 55

PASSING IT ON 60

RETIREMENT 62

Bill Barker 67

DEPARTURE 67

THE TOILET BLOCK 70

THE FLAG 75

James Vernon 80

A PRIVILEGED CHILDHOOD 80

MARGARITA 82

BILL, GORDON and NED 86

MOLLY 89

Darryl Dymock 94

'a' IS LIKE AN APPLE ON A TWIG 94

BEETLEMANIA 98

A GOLDEN THREAD 100

Dave Shearer

DAVE SHEARER'S LIFE began in South Australia in 1945, the youngest of six children. He joined the Army at 16, initially at the Apprentice School at Balcombe, Victoria, and qualified as a Fitter and Turner. In 1966 he was posted to Amberley Airforce Base, Queensland, and spent 15 months operational service in Vietnam. Dave married in 1970, and he and his wife have four children. After his Army discharge in 1971, he worked in Adelaide for Australia Post, followed by employment in South Australia and Queensland with the Federal Government's Lighthouse Service. Subsequently he obtained his Gas Licence and worked within that industry until happily retiring to enjoy his many hobbies.

CHANDLERS HILL ROAD

When you are retired you get asked to do numerous odd jobs. Now, one of these jobs was a request to write my early childhood memories—how could I say no! However, the task has proved very time-consuming and I have little hair remaining on my head from so much scratching,

I best start with my first family house, located 25 or so kilometres south of Adelaide in an area they called Happy Valley. History tells us that there was originally a town of Happy Valley in the early days, but when the government decided to build a freshwater reservoir in the 1890s, the town was swallowed up during construction. So, when I was living there, it was just a rural area with no central town. At that time, our house was built on the south-east boundary of the Happy Valley Reservoir, but now the property falls within the Reservoir boundary. The house was on acreage, with the Reservoir Boundary on one side, which we called the 'Sandy Track', and on the other side, a large vineyard. The house faced Chandlers Hill Road.

Our house was of wooden weatherboard construction with a tiled roof, built in the early 40s, sitting on wooden stumps. Attached to the house was my father's General Store, named the 'Red Star Poultry Farm'. I remember our big kitchen having a wood-fired cooker with a large oven in which my mother cooked many roast chicken and vegetable meals. Plus some tasty desserts. It was my sister's and my job to collect the 'morning's wood' on a daily basis from a nearby paddock so Mum could start the cooker fire each morning. There was a room attached to the kitchen where we all ate our meals, Dad at the head of the table, Mum at the other end, and us six kids down each side. Dad always listened to the 6pm ABC News on the radio, and no one dare spoke.

At bath time, we had a big galvanized metal bath. Saturday night, the girls always went in first, then the next person in line had to go outside to the wood-fired copper boiler to fill up a bucket of hot water and come back in and add it to the bath. So, me being the youngest was always last one in, so when I dived in the water it was nearly inches from the top, like a swimming pool. I still have fond memories of Saturday night baths.

Out the back of the house was an underground fresh water tank, plus Mum's copper boiler she used to do the washing in. There was also a long single wire clothes line with wooden props to support the length of the line, which was more than adequate for the family washing. Now the most important item in the backyard was the toilet. It was a 'long-dropper', way down the back of the property—you needed a cut-lunch and a water bottle to get there! My father had it built facing the east, so you could sit on the full width wooden seat and watch the rising sun in the morning and contemplate life. There was also a small wooden building in the backyard which my older brothers used as a bedroom, and one of the outside walls had overhead cover which we parked Dad's truck under. The best item outback in the yard was my childhood rope swing, which had a wooden seat and two side ropes that you gripped onto while you swung. Many an hour was spent swinging my life away!

Further down the property were fig, nectarine and almond trees, plus a vegetable garden. On the vineyard side was the large chicken house with a closed-in yard; they supplied eggs for sale in the store and our family needs. Down the back paddock was where our milking cow roamed, which was milked every day by my older brother by hand. So, we always had plenty of fresh milk, but we also separated the milk for cream. This process was done with a hand-operated separator. It had a large handle on the side which had to be turned to get the machine working. Those were the days—with desserts covered in 'fresh' cream!

HARRY SHEARER'S GENERAL STORE

Most food items were available plus fruit and veg, petrol and engine oils. There was a hand-operated petrol pump out front of the store. The pump had a large handle on its side, which you operated to draw petrol from the underground tank up into a glass container mounted on the top of the pump. When the quantity was right, you placed the hand piece into the car or motorbike fuel tank and the gravity would let the fuel down. Then Dad had to lift the delivery hose up to his shoulder to let every drop of fuel drain out of the hose.

Running the store was a full-time job as Dad had to travel in to the Adelaide markets to buy produce each week. Remembering that in the early 50s flour and sugar came in large sacks so he had to re-weigh them again into one- and two-pound paper bags before it could go on the store shelf. Now if you knew my father well, you might be able to buy a flagon of port wine too at the right price. These were strategically positioned on the bottom under the main counter. Dad was lucky as the Horndale Winery (Distillery) which opened in 1895, and still operates today, was only one and half kilometres away. And I should add this was why the Happy Valley area was covered with many acres of vineyards—to supply the local wineries.

The Happy Valley Reservoir opened in 1897, and it supplied Adelaide's drinking water, and still does to this day. Back when I was a kid though, this reservoir was my playground, much to the concern of my mother. As you know, when you are five and six years old you can climb brick walls, so the boundary fence was no real challenge, a quick climb over the top or underneath. We walked through the bush down to the water's edge and threw many stones that skimmed and bounced along the top of the water.

However, the biggest interest was the 'Inlet Pipe'. This was a large 1.8 metre diameter pipe which entered the reservoir land not far from our house. The pipe transferred water from Clarendon

Weir, positioned further up in the hills, to top up the water in the Happy Valley Reservoir when required. So being inquisitive kids we would duck our heads down and walk up inside the pipe until it got that dark we couldn't go any further in. Now you ask, when did they turn the valve on to let the water down? As kids we never worried about that, because it was just great fun walking up the inside of the pipe! No wonder my mother raised her voice from time to time and threatened us with no dessert at evening meal. Yes, the reservoir had an unusual attraction to me at this early age.

DARLINGTON

In 1953 Mum and Dad sold the General Store at Happy Valley and we shifted down closer to Adelaide into the suburb of Darlington. This was an area south of Adelaide and at that time was considered the outer edge of suburbia. It was just off Main South Road where the foothills started. Our house was the first house built on the hill face and the local people made the comment 'no one builds a house amongst the box-thorn bushes and the wild olive trees!'

The land was excavated to build our two-tiered wooden and asbestos sheeted house, which ended up with a large front deck. My father and my two older brothers helped fit the external and internal wall sheeting. Mum and Dad lived in a pre-built garage on site and my brothers and myself slept in an old army tent beside the garage. The house was finally completed and we all moved in. There was a large stairway in the middle, which gave access to the two levels. Downstairs in the lounge room were two large windows, one facing north, the other facing the west. At night it gave a great view of the city lights. I remember in heavy winds though, the windows would flex in and out with the pressure placed on them.

Further down the block, Dad built a chook house and a tool shed. Dad was a great gardener, so the whole of the yard was soon covered in cucumbers, tomatoes, potatoes and a variety of melons.

One of my experiences with the tool shed was the day after 'Guy Fawkes Night' or 'Cracker Night'. The following morning, I went out and combed the local park for unexploded crackers and brought them back home into the shed. Then I stripped them open and emptied the powder out into an empty fruit tin. I bet you are asking—how many crackers? Who knows? But I completely filled the tin. Then I placed a new fuse in the top of the tin and took it out into the garden and lit it up. I then raced back into the shed and slammed the door shut! Well... the whole thing went off with such a 'BANG' that it rocked the tool shed.

Mum came running out from the house and shouted something to me but I couldn't hear her because of the ringing in my ears! And just so you know, I never did find the remnants of that fruit tin!

SECONDARY SCHOOL

I followed in the footsteps of my two older brothers and was sent to the Marist Brothers Secondary School at Thebarton, in George Street, just off South Road. The school was a large brick building with five classrooms and high ceilings, with plenty of space between our desks. I say 'space' because my memories of primary school were that our desks were side by side. The blackboard covered right across one wall and the flooring was raised in front to allow the Brothers some height to see down the back of the room. We learnt most subjects but no languages, plus our technical subjects in woodwork and metalwork. I do recall algebra, because I never quite got the reason for learning it in our maths subject, and I will add that in 45 years of work I have never used it—ever!

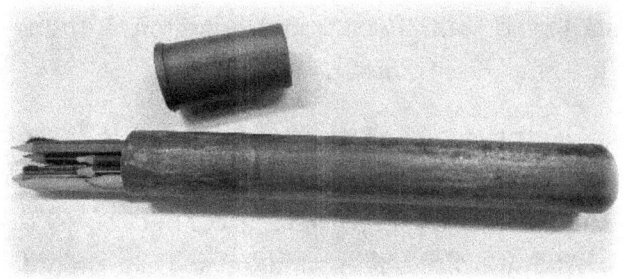

Our trade training workshop was away from the main classrooms in another building. We had woodworking and metalworking sections. No electrical machines in those days as work was performed by handsaws and hand metal folders. I'm proud that I still own my rolled metal pencil case all soldered together. Sport was also a big part of those secondary years. I was not into 'contact' sport, but cricket took up many sports days. Now everybody of that era would remember the physical discipline that was handed out by the teachers, together with the Brothers. Yes, I'm talking about the 'Cane'! Meaning: if you played up or you deliberately did something wrong or against the rules, you had to hold your hand out and have it slapped with a wooden stick or a strip of leather. You just accepted punishment and got on with learning.

My memory recalls another item on our daily supply at school and that was a bottle of milk. The government at that time supplied schools with a third of a pint of fresh milk in glass containers. It really went down well with Mum's rock buns at mid-morning break. Now my final recollection is how I got to and from school, and that was most times by pushbike. The distance was fifteen kilometres each way. Yes, I did get wet in the rain and coming home I had to ride into the headwind. I had a couple of mates I would ride with and at 15 years old it was a challenge on a daily basis. I used South Road from Darlington to Thebarton, but Marion Road had less traffic and was wider.

The skills I learnt at secondary school led me to follow on with training as an adult to get my trade qualifications as a Fitter and Turner. And to this day I still have a connection to the Marist Brothers, as my wife Maree and myself do voluntary work in Cambodia at one of the Brothers School on the outskirts of Phnom Penh. Plus, I still use my trade skills on a day-to-day basis while working at the school. So, my early school training days have come full circle.

JOINING THE ARMY

I suppose the first big change in my life was when I joined the Army at the early age of just sixteen. I applied to do the trade training at the Army Apprentices School at Balcombe, south east of Melbourne. We came from all states and territories around Australia. I remember we had to do numerous examinations, such as English and Maths, to check our highest education level. At my final interview, Mum and Dad came along and spoke on my behalf. I guess as a kid I was always interested in the military. I made a wooden replica of a Thompson sub-machine gun, complete with a removable magazine, I also carved up the leg of my mother's antique wooden chairs to make hand grenades. My mates and I would play war games in amongst the olive trees and down the creek at the back of our house for entertainment after school.

I do remember an incident that fired me up when my mate, who had joined the Navy six months before I was selected for the Army, came home for his first leave. He visited me wearing his newly issued Navy 'walking out' uniform, with 'bell-bottom' pants. They had the seven creases ironed in the lower part of the legs, which represented the seven seas of the world. I was very impressed!

Well, my selection finally came by mail in December 1961, informing me that I would train as a Fitter and Turner for four years—I still have that letter. In addition, the letter stated that we would be leaving from Adelaide for Melbourne by overnight train on 8th January and not to bring any excess clothing except for a spare pair of underpants because we would be issued with heavy woollen ones (with long legs down to your knees) on arrival. Welcome to the Army! This was my transition from adolescence to adulthood, as I had signed up for nine years' service.

Offcuts

Jim Pascoe

Jim Pascoe has spent over sixty years in the Corinda and Oxley area. His entire career was spent in the electrical distribution network, starting his apprenticeship with the Brisbane City Council Electricity Department which became SEQEB, then Energex. He had a varied career in many departments before retiring as Technical Support Officer at the Call Centre. He was a member of the Royal Australian Navy Reserve until he married. He met his wife Janice in Warwick where he spent the majority of his weekends. They have four children and thirteen grandchildren. He has been a member of the *Oxley Men's Shed* since its inception.

A CHANGE OF LIFESTYLE

It certainly was a culture shock for an eleven-year-old moving to Corinda at the end of 1955. I was born at Windsor and spent my early years living beside my grandmother's house in Somerset Street with my family. You might say that Windsor was a near inner suburb of Brisbane. Breakfast Creek was just down at the end of our street and Windsor Oval was just around the corner. Hunter Brother's Island was situated around the corner in Le Geyt Street, and entry was gained by a bridge which we used to jump off as long as the blue cattle guard dogs weren't around. I thought that Windsor was a modern suburb, even though the houses appeared close together, as there were bitumen roads with concrete gutters and the entire suburb was sewered.

To travel to the city was by a tram at the end of the street, and Saturday afternoons were spent at the matinee at the Crystal Palace Picture Theatre. I attended the Windsor State School from prep year until the end of grade five. There were three classes in each grade with over fifty pupils in each class.

When my grandmother died, our family made an historic move to the outer suburb of Corinda. I was sad leaving all my mates and also wondering what lay ahead, but it must have been harder for my fifty-year old dad who had lived all his life in the old house.

Our family moved into a four-bedroom house with a sleep-out, dining room, sewing room, lounge room, kitchen and a bathroom with, yes, a chip water-heater. Located in the back corner of the backyard was, believe it or not, the outhouse. This structure came with a front trellis with its obligatory grapevine—whose grapes were very sour—and a loquat tree at the side. The sanitary man from Hunter Brothers came weekly with a new can with fresh sawdust and removed the old one. This was a novelty to us and we always hoped that we wouldn't be caught in there when the dunny man arrived.

Our house was located in Lynne Grove Avenue, just one house away from the railway line to Ipswich. There were also three shunting lines which ended at sets of buffers opposite our house. Another shock to the system was the fact that our street was dirt and there were no gutters. The bread and also the ice were delivered by horse and cart but the baker's cart had pneumatic tyres for comfort.

Instead of travelling to the city by tram in fifteen minutes, we now caught a steam train which took thirty minutes. This was a great adventure with so many stations. It also travelled over the Brisbane River at Chelmer and through a tunnel before reaching town.

I began grade six at Corinda State School and it didn't take long to meet mates from nearby streets. There was always something to do after school and we all used to wander all over the neighbourhood as long as we were home by five o'clock. Things were certainly different all those years ago, and we could cross the railway lines and go up to Montrose Home, then climb down the cliff and swim in the river or take our trolleys and race them down beside St Aidan's Girls' School. Playing in the bush below the Fort and picking their mangoes, when they were in season, was a great pastime as well.

Have you ever heard of the *Haunto?* This was the area which now encompasses the Corinda State High School but in those days was a place of adventure. You could always obtain a feed of mullet or mud crabs in Oxley Creek, that is, if you weren't swimming in there. There was a mass of lantana which was great for playing in, apart from the scratches. There were also stands of Rangoon cane for fishing rods, and also bamboo which was used for making bird nesting boxes. One great yabby spot was located in the creek near where the Dunlop Pool now stands and another was in Nixon Park, Oxley. The end of Cliveden Avenue was the best place to trap Double bars, Zebra and Bull Finches and Greenies.

We all had aviaries for our birds but only one mate kept pigeons. He used to obtain them from the Corinda Shire Hall which is now the library. He used to soak wheat in methylated spirits and then spread it in the gutters and then wait until they became drunk on the feed. He took them home and, after a couple of weeks, sold them as homing pigeons. They always returned to the hall so he always had a steady supply of pigeons for sale.

Even though times were hard for us in the early years, the experiences that we enjoyed didn't cost anything and all of us could always amuse ourselves with what we made. The only time that we needed money was to go to the pictures or when it was time for the Ekka and how that was obtained will have to wait until another time.

LOVE IS IN THE AIR

It was on Friday, the eighteenth of December, 1964 when my cousin Pam and I, along with my mate Ross and his cousin Janice were walking along Palmerin Street on our way to see the Christmas Parade in Warwick. I had taken Pam out on a couple of occasions and she was a mate of Janice and worked at her father's garage in King Street.

As I was walking along hand in hand with Pam, Ross, who was not backward in coming forward, said, 'It's not very romantic walking along holding hands with your cousin. Why don't we swap?'

We did and I have, since then, been holding hands with Janice for the last fifty-five years.

That was the start of our romance and I wondered how her father would take it as he was the one from whom I received 'the Order of the Boot' on the previous New Year's Eve in 1963. I don't know what happened but her mum and dad must have realised that I wasn't such a bad chap after all and I was permitted to take Janice out. This was also received very well by both her auntie and uncle and gran at the farm as she was one of their favourites.

Initially I would stop at her house on my way to Dalveen on a Friday night and drive down on a Saturday night to take her to the pictures or to the Dalveen dances. If we went to the dances, I would drive over a hundred miles for the night. When we went to the Warwick theatre we would be chaperoned by her young brother, Nigel. I would shout him into the pictures. I didn't know until years later that he was given money by his parents but he saved it to buy cigarettes.

I could never sneak up on Janice on a Friday night as my Morris Minor 1000 would cause interference to the television reception and she would know it was me pulling up at the front gate.

True love blossomed and I partnered her to the Warwick Caledonian Ball on the eighteenth of June 1965. As Warwick had a large Scottish heritage, this event was always well received by the community. The kilts that the partners wore were of the Black Watch Tartan and loaned by the Scots College. There were five debutantes presented to the clan chieftain that night and Janice was selected to cut the cake and I had the honour of making the presentation speech.

To complete the night, I was given the keys to a brand new Valiant sedan to drive Janice home after the ball finished. The only downside to that was that there were protective plastic covers placed on the seats and anyone who has ever worn a kilt will appreciate how cold it could be on the back of one's legs in winter time.

Offcuts

The romance increased and I no longer stayed at Dalveen, except during the holidays, and had now progressed to staying at her house every weekend. This was a more economical proposition as I didn't travel so far. Janice would wake me up at 4:30am of a Monday morning with tea and toast and then I would drive to Brisbane and arrive in time to go to work.

As Janice worked every Saturday morning at Doyle's Pharmacy my time was now spent taking her mother shopping in town. Her parents owned Bruce Mitchell's Garage and, as well as having a motor mechanic shop, they also sold Valiant, Dodge vehicles and Fiat tractors. One activity of a Saturday afternoon was to attend all the local shows in the district and display all the new vehicles and take part in the grand parade and then bring the vehicles home afterwards.

Towards the end of 1966, I was attending the Tuesday Royal Australian Navy Reserve training night which was held at *HMAS Moreton* in New Farm. At stand easy, I said to my old high school mate Merv that I was going to ask Janice's parents for her hand in marriage on the next weekend. I was now a tradesman and believed that I could afford to be married.

He said, 'Well, if you are, then so will I.' His girlfriend lived in Toowoomba.

On the Saturday morning, at the breakfast table, Janice said something like: 'When we get married, we'll have such and such.' Her mother said, 'Jim hasn't asked yet, so that I can say no.' That was my cue and I quickly asked, 'Well, can I?' Her mother didn't know what to say and then said, 'Ask Dad.'

He was at that time slowly eating his rice bubbles so I turned to him and again said, 'Can I?' He hadn't heard the previous conversation and looked at me and said, 'What?'

I said, 'Marry Janice.' Having caught him on the hop, he nearly choked on his rice bubbles and hopelessly looked at his wife for support. 'What do you think, Mum?'

'I don't know, what do you think, Dad?'

'Er, um, ok, you can marry her,' he replied, and then it was kisses and handshakes all around.

I'll bet that he didn't envisage that the person that he kicked up the behind would come back as a future son-in-law two years later.

As luck would have it, my sister was getting married on the next weekend and I brought Janice down to Brisbane and we were able to purchase the engagement ring on that Saturday morning before the wedding, but we weren't going to tell anyone until later.

My Dad was the first one to notice the ring and was 'over the moon' as he had a soft spot for my new fiancée.

Driving back to Warwick, we then made a quick trip to Dalveen where we informed all at the farm, as well as gran, about what we had done. We were officially engaged on the eighteenth of February 1966. Janice's sister Vona had been married in 1965 and we decided that we would wait twelve months before our big event.

Of course both Ross and Pam were in the bridal party—with Pam being the chief bridesmaid and Ross, my best mate, as the best man. The wedding would be held in the St Andrew's Presbyterian

Church, Warwick, on the eighteenth of February, 1967, but that's another story.

A DROVING TRIP

In 1986 Ross and his wife Marg were leasing a two-and-a-half thousand hectare property called *Mt Pleasant Station* near Mingoola in New South Wales. They had been there for eight years and were now in the process of moving to a newly leased property called *Wongalea* that was approximately 130 kilometres away and south of Yetman.

Ross was my best mate and also Janice's cousin, and had been the best man at our wedding. We had always been close and always tried to get together as much as possible and help him at the farm.

They were sheep farmers and had over four hundred ewes and approximately eighteen hundred wethers. All the sheep were of the superfine wool type and threw a heavy fleece when shorn.

Ross had decided that, instead of trucking the entire mob to the new property, he would only truck the ewes and then drive the wethers down the stock route which paralleled the Bruxner Highway. By doing this, he would save leasing fees and also the grass on the new property.

As I was working in Brisbane, we organised with him that we would leave home very early on the Saturday morning of the June long weekend and meet up with them at their overnight camp at the Bonshaw Weir. The Bonshaw Pub used to be situated nearby but it burned down on New Year's Eve in 1998. It was a great little pub and the wall above the bar had been adorned with the mouths of the Murray Cod that had been caught nearby.

Being winter, it was cold when we got there and it then decided to rain. So Janice and our children drove down with Marg to the next overnight stop, which was to be on the banks of the Dumaresq River near Texas. They all set up the camp there while we prepared for the drive. Marg's parents were along for the trip and carried out all the cooking.

There were three of us on horseback and I was 'lucky' enough to lead the appaloosa colt 'Cactus' whom, I might say, didn't like this arrangement at all and kept pulling back on the halter most of the time. My horse was my old favourite 'Stoney', another appaloosa. He had never been 'broken in' and didn't have a mean bone in his body and the only thing that you had to look out for were rabbit holes as he had a pet aversion to them.

I was glad to have had my wet weather gear with me in the car and it was quickly donned before we moved off. There is nothing worse than sitting on a wet saddle for a full day in wet weather.

That first day was miserable with the cold rain pouring down. My hands were blue and numb from the cold and even the emus looked at us as though we were mad when we rode past them. We were.

At the end of the day, a temporary holding yard for the sheep and horses was set up and we then drove to our night stop.

Ross had picked out a couple of 'killers' that were brought back with us to camp and it was my job to butcher them. It was always my job to sharpen the butcher's knives as Ross was hopeless with them even though he could sharpen anything else.

Offcuts

I despatched the sheep near the bank of the Dumaresq River where the sand was deep and where it was easy to dig a hole to bury the skins and intestines in. Having done the deed and the carcases skinned and dressed, they were then covered and hung in an adjacent tree making sure that nothing could get to them overnight.

After a nice warm bush shower and a couple of well-earned rums, we sat down to tea around the nice warm fire before finally traipsing off to bed. We didn't make it a long night as we were all tired.

Waking up to another cold and wet day, the first job after a hot breakfast was to butcher the sheep. The carcases had been frozen overnight and it was quite an easy job to cut them up and pack them away in the Eskys. Driving back to the mob, we found that they were still well settled and after saddling the horses and taking down the night fence we began the next stage of our drive. It was a better day than the day before, and the mob walked well.

There was one young wether that Ross called 'Limpy'. As a lamb he was tail docked, ringed and given an injection in the leg which must have been inserted into a muscle. After that, for the rest of his life, he walked stiff-legged. He eventually died of old age as Ross didn't have the heart to kill him for meat after his wool-growing days were over. He said that if he had been good and strong enough to walk all the way to *Wongalea*, then he had earned the right to live to a ripe old age.

It is amazing how much fauna and flora there is to be seen while quietly riding along a stock route. As the rain had stopped and as it began to dry out, the kangaroos began to make their appearance and even some emus followed us for some time. There were even a couple of koalas in some trees that we saw as we rode past.

The mob was fenced near our camp that night and it was easy keeping a watch on them. The cooks had been extremely busy and when we all sat down they presented us with a lovely meal of roast lamb and vegetables with a dessert following. Never had anything tasted so delicious as, having been in the saddle all day, we all had a very large appetite.

The weather had cleared and, although it was still cool and also being our last night, we all settled down around the campfire where a good time was had by all.

The next morning was fine and clear and the camp was broken down and all the gear was packed away before the mob was again on the move toward Yetman. It was only a short day for us as we had to make our way back to Brisbane—but not before calling into Stanthorpe where Janice's parents now lived.

It had been a great, although tiring, weekend but one that we would not have missed. After our departure, the drive took two more weeks of travel to reach the new property, where they were met with some of the ewes beginning to lamb.

When we made our next visit to their new property, we took the obligatory coffee essence, Malibu, orange juice, celery, cheese whiz (Ross loved cheese whiz and celery), and the much promised bottle of Bundy rum.

Of course, Ross always had his priorities in the right order as, sitting on the kitchen table and laid out in order of use were all the butcher's knives waiting patiently for me to put an edge on them. That was certainly going to cost him a rum when I had finished.

Offcuts

Bill Thirkill

Bill Thirkill grew up in Brisbane and did an apprenticeship to become a plumber. He moved to France to do skydiving in the world championships, then became a coach tour manager, where he met his wife Fran. They were engaged in Israel and married in England, then moved to New Zealand, and finally to Australia. They have three children. On his return to Australia, Bill took up plumbing again, but retired at age 60 when his son Peter took over the plumbing business. Eventually Bill went back to tour driving, this time in Africa. He has driven coach tours through 54 countries.

INDIA 1964

At age 23 through circumstances I happened to be in India and very short of money. I travelled to Madras by train 3rd class from New Delhi, having to change trains many times. At one place in the middle of India I happened to meet some wonderful people who were running a hospital for very poor people, which was paid for by a US volunteer agency called *American Peace Corps*. These people were so nice and dedicated and vital for the poor people, several using iron lungs to try to overcome the effects of polio.

I had to leave, as I had to get to Madras within a couple of days, so it was back into 3rd class on the train. Which meant a compartment for eight fitting about twenty, as seats were squatted on and bags in between, and me on the port [luggage] rack. At each station the beggars would come aboard. Outside each station I could get some food through the window served on a banana leaf, always some curry and rice, which was quite nice but gave me diarrhoea.

After my job was done I returned to the *Peace Corps* hospital because I wanted to help the nurses and others, and for this they were very grateful. Part of my duties was helping those with polio and particularly a young lady about my age whom I got to really like. I spent much time with her teaching her English and holding her to stop falls but, to my absolute sorrow, she took a serious turn and passed away in my arms.

This was so distressing to me that I had to move on.

I took a train to Bombay and checked into the *Red Shield* hotel, which I had stopped at before, and set about working out how I could get out of India. Maybe crew on a cargo ship, but would see what I could do. As I was short of rupees, I was looking to earn some and the Bollywood movies people were looking for whites to play the part of a British army officer in their movie. But the role was so anti-British that they could not get Brits to do it but, as I had no scruples that way and needed the money, I took on the role.

In the movie I played the part of a British army captain in charge of a torture squad, and we were trying to locate a fellow called Zabash. We had his beautiful wife captured so she was required to tell us his whereabouts and she refused. I'm sure all Bombay could hear her screams as I ordered the squad to give her volts of electricity. You see, I was a really bad bugger, and the Indians must have hated the Brits much more once they saw my movie, but I think I should have got an Oscar.

In between movie jobs I enjoyed going south by train to Goa. It's a really beautiful place and, as it was a Portuguese colony for hundreds of years, was mainly Christian and had many little white churches with coconut trees all around. Hundreds of people would help pull in the fish nets.

To come back to Bombay I used a ship called *Rohades,* an incredibly old ship—black hull, fawn top and rust all over—but at evening the bugs came out and the passengers scratched all night.

My best friends were a guy from Kenya and a Brit who spoke so frightfully well. He just loved my Australian accent, and we did everything together. Mainly the fun thing was to visit the brothels where we could buy beer, as it was illegal elsewhere. We met the most beautiful women—most would be carrying some dreaded disease but great to talk to. There we met the crew of the cargo ships and could ask for a job, but they all seemed to be heading east and I needed to go west.

There was a movie theatre about a kilometre from my digs and one night I decided to go, as a movie in English was on and I needed that. As it turned out I was the only white in the theatre. The theatre was really beautiful, the seats lay back and the screen was set up quite high.

The movie—*The Sound of Music.* Wow, what a place to see it and the Indians showed all the emotions that Australians would show and enjoyed it as much as we do.

On returning to my digs at 11pm all the footpaths were taken up by people sleeping, some families with home-made stretchers and most just on the bitumen walkway with a sheet or two, rats in between. I walked on the road.

Eventually I left India and went by ship to Suez, Egypt, and caught a bus to Cairo.

AFGHANISTAN 1964

After I crossed the border into Afghanistan from Iran with my two buses, I found that the road was even worse than those we had been on. The tyres were suffering, things started breaking, I lost my brakes and the accelerator cable came off. Then I got a puncture. As I had already used my spare and the other bus had too, I decided to jack up the bus, take the wheel off, then prop the bus up and take another wheel off and give it to the other driver for a spare and send him to the next town, Herat, for some new tyres.

As the bus was on chocks we could not wait inside as it was a bit precarious. The wind was blowing and really cold as it was late in the afternoon. Then I saw a ditch about fifty metres away, which was about three metres deep and about eight metres across. I suggested we all wait there out of the wind. The land was flat and dry and dusty.

Some time later, maybe an hour, we were startled when we looked up to see about thirty men with big beards looking down at us. My ladies were really scared and all looked at me to sort this, as western women were unseen in this part of the world.

What to do? They were a very scary bunch, all wearing long sheepskin coats with the wool side in, and quite a fierce look about them. I thought about the situation for a bit, then climbed out of the ditch and shook hands with every one of them, somehow managing a friendly smile while doing so. It worked, broke the ice and they all smiled back and we became friends. All the passengers climbed out and were amazed to see nearby at least fifty camels, hundreds of people and lots of black tents. We had come across a nomad tribe from Turkmenistan and they were really nice to us. We sampled their food and they ours, and we met their kids and camels. All really nice.

Our other bus arrived, so we said goodbye to our new friends and then headed to Herat. I really loved Herat as it was a very old town that the world had forgotten, and there were very few cars—I only saw one. But there were a few very decorated trucks and mostly horse-drawn vehicles. I really loved hearing a taxi going past at night as the bell above the horse's head would ring. I thought we were in the twenties. I loved the queue for bread as it was a hole about two metres deep in the street with a fire and a guy slapping the dough against the side to cook flat bread, which our girls put Vegemite on. He was nearly as cooked as the bread.

On leaving Herat we headed south and were amazed to find a beautiful bitumen road. Apparently the Russians had built it, and the Americans built the bridges. Seemed a bit suspicious to me. This was the first sealed road since Tehran and so good to whizz along at a good speed.

After dark we didn't see a boom gate at the border for another state and my second driver crashed into it. Bugger. I became the responsible person, being the one in charge. So I was arrested and the buses parked till we could sort this out. I was brought into a large tent with many soldiers and waited—all night. I could not speak Farsi nor they English but we got along very well. During the night I was able to ask many questions such as, 'What is the difference between Sunni and Shiite Muslims? What about the beads carried by many?'

They wanted to know if I was a Christian or a Catholic. All this was explained without words and I had a great night. The commanding officer arrived at 6 am. By then we were all good friends and they convinced him to let me go.

At this time a war broke out between India and Pakistan, and I knew we might have trouble ahead but we carried on to Kandahar. And on to Kabul. Kabul was of interest, as there all the women wore the full burka, mostly light blue with net at the eyes. But my worry was that I could no longer enter India through Pakistan. What to do? Decision made: I should sell one of my buses, put my people on a plane to New Delhi and catch a train to Madras. Sounds easy. Not so.

I was quite surprised to see the name ROYAL AFGHANISTAN AIRLINES. Wow, they are royal. Interesting. I needed one of their planes. The problem was that the bus I had to sell was on my passport, which meant I could not leave without it. This had to be sorted, not easy, but finally these problems were overcome. I could sell the bus. But the old plane was a problem. It was a DC4 and had been used on the Berlin airlift a few years before. There were then more problems, but to cut a long story short (because I was a bit naughty and won't tell here what I did), we did get to New Delhi. But my job was to get them to Madras, a couple of thousand kilometres south. Another story. But I left India about ten kilograms lighter months later.

ISRAEL 1966/67

As the coach tour leader, I arrived back in Jordan from Kuwait and Iraq with four passengers who had chosen to go with me to get another vehicle. I then met up with the tour group that I had left there a few days earlier, and started the tour again by taking them to Bethlehem. They were quite shocked to find that all the holy Christian sites were nicely looked after by Muslim people, but were okay with it when I explained how there were so many Christian people with different views—like Greek Orthodox who seemed to hate the Russian Orthodox, and so on.

In Jerusalem we walked the Via Dolorosa and were happy to know that, even though shops were run by the three religions, they all got on well and manned each other's shops when absent for attending services: Muslims on Friday, Jews on Saturday, and Christians on Sunday. All good. It was a surprise that the Mount of Olives still had trees from two thousand years ago.

After we had covered Jerusalem quite well, one of my passengers requested we have a look at Jericho. So I decided to do that but when we arrived and drove through town I could see trouble. The Palestinians looked angry, thinking we may be Jews. At the end of town I turned the bus to get out but too late. I told all my passengers to lie on the floor as I thought they would shoot at us but luckily they didn't. I had many windows broken by rocks, but no injuries.

This was a problem as we were to go through Switzerland in a couple of weeks in December—snow and ice. So I had to fix the windows. There were no bus windows available, so I decided to try making some. I scored a sheet of Perspex and found someone to cut it for me, and I and one of my passengers fitted the windows. All good.

But things were starting to heat up. It was November 1966 and problems were quite noticeable as the Israeli people bombed

Hebron quite close by. I organised to cross into Israel early the next day but did not know where the checkpoint was. So I decided to find it at about 8 am the night before as I now had two vehicles, with one of our passengers driving the other, and I didn't want to get it wrong.

I did find the crossing point but I didn't know that the vehicle we picked up from Kuwait that I was driving was the same colour and make as the ones the Israeli Army drive. The Arab guy manning the gate panicked and pointed his gun at us. I will never forget the look of terror on his face and how much he was shaking when we were driving full speed in reverse as he was trying to shoot at us. Fortunately, he was a lousy shot.

In Israel we stopped in Haifa and, just as well, because the Egyptians bombed Nazareth. However we carried on and went to the Dead Sea and had a swim and did all the must-do things you do when visiting that country. As Israel is a really big diamond processing country, there were many shops selling them and I went into one with Fran, my Favourite Passenger, and bought her an engagement ring, which she accepted with a smile.

We were then to take the ship to Greece but found that they had loaded a big tanker onto the front deck where our two vehicles were to be. A problem. We then managed to get a place on a ship leaving Tel Aviv with room on the deck. They had a large net on the ground which I drove onto and the ship's crane lifted it onto the deck.

We went via Cyprus and on to Greece. I showed as many sights as I could around Athens, then drove on to Olympia and north to Igoumenitsa. Then it was across the Adriatic Sea to Brindisi, and north through Italy, where we spent some time in Florence. After that it was through the Simplon Pass into Switzerland where we drove through a blizzard—a very difficult drive. From there we headed to France but didn't have chains to cross the mountains to Lyon, and after using ropes around the wheels to no avail, I turned back and went through Dijon.

Following a brief stop in Paris, it was finally back to London. After lots of sleep I found a nice registry office and married Fran, a Kiwi girl. She had been my passenger for eighteen weeks and through twenty-eight countries, coped well with a lot of drama, and she still wears the ring fifty-four years later. I have driven her throughout Australia and Africa and she still loves it. Our three children all live close by in Brisbane.

ATLANTIC STORM 1967

In 1967 Fran and I were living in London but we really wanted to go to New Zealand so I would be able to meet Fran's parents, brother and sister and friends. On enquiring with QANTAS, we found flying was really expensive so we started looking for a ship to take us. First we tried P & O. They had a ship going via USA and Canada, a long and expensive trip. But we found an Italian company, Cogidar line, that had a much smaller migrant ship, *Flavia*. It was a shorter trip at about half the price.

We left Southampton about the first of March, 1967, on the 20,000-ton ship *Flavia* with about 1500 passengers, many of them Italians. We were to head south-west into the Atlantic, past the Azores and south to the Caribbean Sea through the Panama Canal and across the Pacific to Auckland.

All went well for the first day, then the sea started getting rough. The passengers, mostly Italian migrants paying ten pounds for the voyage, were so sick that, by the next morning with the sea really wild, out came the rosary beads. The colour of the water was a very dark blue and, as the ship's bow would plunge into the huge waves completely covering it, the stern would come out of the water, leaving the propellers spinning. But as the stern plunged back into the water it shook the whole ship very badly. All access to the decks was blocked off, and to move within the ship required ropes to go hand over hand, sometimes uphill, sometimes down. At the dining room all the tablecloths were wet to stop plates flying off. I had a bottle of whisky in the wardrobe, and one wave hit so hard the bottle banged the door open allowing the whisky to escape and smash on the floor. The storm was incredibly noisy but, to add to the racket, there was the crashing of plates. The galley was above our cabin and everything was breaking.

Fran became very sick, she was pregnant at the time. I think the baby inside was also sick. Most of the passengers and crew were sick also. We pushed on through the force 12 storm, then the engines conked out and we were at the mercy of the huge waves. In the distance we saw the Azores Islands, but we drifted away from them, which was very lucky. Two days later, there was a wonderful sound as the engines started and we headed for the Caribbean. The ocean became calmer, the Islands of the Dominican Republic passed, then through the Caribbean on to Panama City—not a very nice place. The canal is very interesting with many locks to go over the mountains.

On to Tahiti. The Pacific Ocean was so calm, the only excitement was the occasional water spout. In Tahiti we enjoyed the town

Papeete. We went around the island in a truck delivering milk and coconuts to houses. Lovely. Then on to New Zealand.

All went well for the rest of the voyage, and we had a really nice time as the Italian crew entertained as well as performed their ship duties. They were really good. We crossed the International Date Line on 13th April 1967—so never saw 14th April, and eventually arrived at Auckland. We took a bus to New Plymouth and I met Fran's parents. I am sure that they were not delighted with her choice of husband. They were not happy that we married in a registry office and insisted we wed again, this time in a church.

Baby Diane was born four months later in Australia. As years went by, we found Diane was very susceptible to motion sickness. When driving we would have to stop and let her walk for a while, even short trips like home to school was sometimes a problem. I blamed the Atlantic.

Offcuts

Michael Reynolds

Michael Reynolds' mother died on the day he was born in November 1944, and he was brought up by his Aunt Kathleen and her husband Jack. He received his early education in Rosewood and Ipswich and went to high school in Toowoomba. At school he was involved in rugby, athletics and swimming, and went on to represent Ipswich in rugby league. After school Michael started work in the insurance industry, first with SGIO (later *Suncorp*) and subsequently with *Queensland Treasury*. In 1964 he married Gail, and they had three children. They initially lived in Ipswich, then Oxley. Gail died from cancer in 2013, and Michael now lives in a retirement village at Oxley.

MAJESTIC THEATRE

The street light was on. It was a dim light—but it was on. The theatre was in darkness. The wind had increased. What had happened was that the film was finished. I don't remember the name of the picture now. And at that time movies were referred to as 'the pictures'. I sat in the front seats, which were comfortable. They were made of wood frames and canvas bags. The back of the theatre had good covered seating. I thought it was a great place because it was named the *Majestic Theatre*.

I was in my early teens, and on this night I had fallen asleep, and the theatre manager woke me and told me to go home. This was part of an arrangement between my aunt and uncle and the manager (the theatre owner/operator). The other part was that I was to behave myself at the theatre. At the time, my aunt and uncle ran the *Rosewood Hotel*, and they reared me throughout their life.

Out the front door it was dark and windy and there was an eerie feeling about the place. I checked as far as I could. The *Rosewood Hotel*, where I lived, was approximately 100 metres from the *Majestic Theatre*. There was some talk that a ghost had taken up residence there too.

The best chance I had was to start and run on the crown of the road. The risky parts were where it was very dark, and I was hoping that I didn't trip and fall over. Off I dashed. The front entry to their hotel was a large decorated door, usually locked after business hours. It was left unlocked when I went to the pictures.

My target was to be under the blankets (so nobody could get me) without delay. I think I heard some movement in my aunt and uncle's bedroom, but I soon fell into a deep sleep.

My aunt, Kathleen, and her husband John (Jack) Heenan, became my guardians after my mother Margaret died on the same day I was born, 28 November 1944, due to complications after the birth. From this time, they were affectionately known to me as Mum and Jack. My father, Patrick (Boy) Reynolds kept in touch with me throughout my formative years. Kathleen Heenan died on 28 September 1986, aged 67 years, and is buried in the Laidley Cemetery beside Jack, who died on 1 March 1973, aged 73 years.

Kathleen and Jack were publicans and owned and operated hotels in Laidley and Rosewood. Thus I spent most of my early years living in hotels. A drawback in hotel living for me was that

Kathleen often became aware of my movements (indiscretions) in the town through information shared with her by customers. One of these events was at the local swimming hole.

THE SWIMMING HOLE

When I was growing up in Rosewood, I was fascinated by the plant items that accumulated on the banks of the branch of the river near the old swimming hole in the creek. At the time a large number of trees of varying sizes, types and colours, were growing on the banks.

There was one tree (or part of a tree) that was used as a jump-off point into the water. As we had no idea of what was under the water, diving had to be a shallow dive. So we had a type of diving, probably what you would call a duck-dive.

One day I was out on the branch, and I was intending to have a swim. I didn't see my mate Greg was already in the water, moving towards me. I did a duck dive and only when I came in contact with him did I realise Greg was in the swimming hole.

There was a free flow of blood from Greg's arm, and we immediately got him on to the bank. We had some towels and wrapped them around his arm. Of course, in those times in the 1950s, we didn't have any first aid equipment or ambulance assistance for Greg.

When he settled, we got him on to my bike. The blood was still flowing but not as much. We were thankful that he had no serious injuries. Afterwards, nothing was said to us, which was unusual.

THE BOY FROM ROSEWOOD

I received my early education in Rosewood and Ipswich, and then completed secondary school as a boarder at Downlands College in Toowoomba. In 1961 I commenced working in the insurance industry at the *State Government Insurance Office (Queensland)*. *The State Government Insurance Office*, better known as the SGIO, later became *Suncorp Insurance*. My insurance career with Suncorp continued until 1999 when I accepted a redundancy offer. I wasn't ready for retirement at the time, however, and started a second insurance career with *Queensland Treasury*. There I had the responsibility of establishing and managing a self-insurance scheme for Queensland Government departments and other selected agencies.

I have never been far from sport and at school was involved in rugby, athletics and swimming. As a teenager and young adult, I represented Ipswich in rugby league and retired from the sport in 1966. In the last three seasons to 1966, I played in the Bulimba Cup competition which was then the premier rugby league competition between Brisbane, Ipswich and Toowoomba. A high point during this period was representing Ipswich against the touring Great Britain side in 1966. From 1962 to 1964 I was a member of *Currumbin Surf Life Saving Club*, and the lifesaving club duties and competitions were the summer sporting activities. Over the years I've been involved in other sporting activities such as marathon running—having completed 14 marathons in the 1984–1998 period, and competitive touch football in the 1976–1981 period when I again represented Ipswich and South East Queensland at various touch football carnivals.

I was married to Gail Grayson on 8 August 1964 at Ipswich. Gail was a beautician at *David Jones* and then moved to ladies fashion retail and spent many enjoyable and interesting years with the *Sportsgirl* company. Gail's working career was put on hold during the child-rearing years and then there were periods of part-time work subject to needs of the children. Gail was then with *Christian Supplies,* a religious books, vestments and items retailer. The clergy, many of whom were known to her, were among the clientele and she enjoyed the contact with them and other interesting and, in some cases, extraordinary people.

Following our marriage Gail and I lived in Ipswich, and in 1971 moved to Oxley in Brisbane. We raised three children: Bradley, Adam and Nicole. In the 2000s Gail was diagnosed with blood cancer and we were fortunate to have her with us until 2013.

POSTSCRIPT

Following Gail's funeral, the family naturally experienced a period of sadness. Fortunately it did not last for long, and we had to support the children. The family rallied to each other, and by the end of 2016 we were managing things. I am a member of *Oxley Men's Shed* and the members were very good to me. I owe them a vote of thanks.

It became apparent that I would have to consider the future to better manage our family assets. The decision was made to sell the family home, and I moved into a retirement village not far away. Life is very busy...

Offcuts

Trevor Ross Armstrong

TREVOR ROSS ARMSTRONG HAS LED a worthwhile life surrounded by three brothers and three sisters. He had a loving mother with ten siblings, and guiding father managing a mixed dairy/ crop /beef farm while serving many grateful fresh-milk customers from early morning—every day of the year, through droughts, diseases, fire and floods. He developed practical, integrated weed management programs via the *Alan Fletcher Research Station*. Trevor has won *Best Allround Sportsman* and many other awards, but is content to volunteer as Bush/Creek Carer to rehabilitate degraded areas to benefit native and local communities for future generations.

FROM MILK RUNNER TO WEEDS RESEARCH AGRONOMIST

I feel blessed that my background experiences—from a simple country upbringing on a Bremer River floodplain dairy farm near Rosewood to many adventures in Ipswich, Brisbane and beyond—has led me to living a purposeful city life helping family, friends and teams of others in local communities towards taking up opportunities for becoming sustainable stewards around our precious Earth.

I was born on 9th April, 1948, a few minutes after my twin sister, Heather Belle, in the General Hospital, Ipswich, Queensland. I had an elder sister, Joycelyn Beatrice, born on 24th February

1938; elder brother, Roy Thomas, born on 22nd February 1941, and brother, Darrell Bruce born on 10th January, 1945. Later, my younger brother, Gregory John, was born on 9th December 1951, and younger sister, Meryl Anne, was born on 17th February 1954. Our father, Leslie Arthur ARMSTRONG, was born on 31st August 1907, in Ebenezer, and our mother, Beatrice Warner née ELLIOTT was born on 16th December 1919, in Amberley. They were married on 21st August 1937, in the Congregational Church, Amberley, and lived in a new home my Dad had built on 180 acres (72 ha) of land that Arthur had bought in 1926 (the same year his mother died of a heart attack/Myocarditis/ Syncope). His father, Tom, died on 19th June 1951 at Ebenezer, of Senile/Cardio-vascular degeneration/ Bronchitis. Both are buried at Stone Quarry Cemetery, Ebenezer. The farm was cleared and cropped with corn etc. near the *Seven Mile (Creek) Bridge* on the Rosewood-Amberley Road, across the Bremer River from where Dad had grown up at *'Spring Hill',* Ebenezer.

My father's father, Thomas (Tom) ARMSTRONG was born on 7th February, 1869, in the County of Churchill, Ipswich (with his twin sister who died at birth), and married at Wesleyan Church, Ebenezer, in 1892 to Eliza Ida BERGMANN who was born on 18th January, 1870, at Jeebropilly Parish, Ipswich. Tom and Ida first lived in a newly built home on Portion 35, Parish of Jeebropilly, N.E. corner of Ebenezer Rd (now Armstrong Lane). After his father, John ARMSTRONG, died in 1895, Tom took over his c. 500 acres (200 ha) property about 1900. This house was shifted over to the top of *'Spring Hill',* enlarged and joined to the existing c. 1878-built 'Gran's House', where Tom's mother, Harriett née MILLER, lived until her death in 1916.

The same *'Back Flat'* Portion 35 was originally bought at Harriett's insistence, even though it was melon-holey and required many woody weeds, mainly native Brisbane Blue Gum *(Eucalyptus teretecornis)* suckers, to be controlled for efficient grazing use. In 1980—after my father's death on 26th December, 1979, just two days after my only son, Andrew Ross was born—I inherited this same Portion 35 of c. 100 acres (40 ha) and later sold it to my brother Greg's eldest son, Michael Gregory ARMSTRONG, who built his new marriage home on this same corner site for his family farm complex.

My first memories were after my 3rd birthday when Mum scrubbed up my twin sister and me from a tub of warm water on our sunny eastern veranda, dressed us in our best clothes and told us she was taking us to Rosewood Congregational Church Sunday School's Kindergarten, 'So we could get used to mixing with other potential class mates before we were due to start school.' (School was a two-mile lift or walk, and later bike ride, west). We lived on this *7 Mile (Creek/ Bridge)* dairy farm—from which Dad rose as early as 12.30 am during World War 2 to milk dual purpose *Learton Red Poll Stud* cows—helped by Mum while he had breakfast. Dad drove seven miles, across Amberley RAAF Base (later *Redex* and other flood etc. detours around obstacles) to deliver fresh milk from 10-gallon cans via tap and pint to (cheaper by the) gallon measures checked by inspectors into billy cans. Grateful customers had their own jugs, containers etc. and paid cash, with our money bags for change, there and from *3 Mile Bridge* to *One Mile* (Leichhardt) and beyond West Ipswich, every day of the year, before 240 Volt power and refrigeration: 'As the early bird gets the customers before breakfast and without middle men taking dairy farmers' profits.'

When Dad sold this dairy farm and milk run in early 1957 to fulfil his dream of retiring by the time he turned 50, we bought and our whole family moved to *Scotts of Ipswich* [a large manufacturing company] large home and air raid shelter block at 24 Brisbane Road, East Ipswich. But the Victorian dairy family who took over Dad's business could not keep up the promised repayments— even after depleting a whole large hayshed of fodder—so we ended up having to re-possess and arrange share-farmer families to work the dairy farm while Dad travelled to and from home and delivered milk to depleted customer numbers (due to bad rumours), plus cream to *Booval Butter Factory* daily. Darrell and I would ride our push bikes to the corner of Clay and Omar Streets, West Ipswich, and run to meet Dad before 7am on the *1 Mile Bridge*, corner of Old Toowoomba Rd and Lobb St—as, by then, the RAAF had blocked access across their airstrip. A customer asked what I'd like to do when I left school. I answered, 'Become an agricultural scientist,' which surprised her and others, but helped me work towards achieving this purposeful life goal.

Darrell attended Ipswich State High School (ISHS) and I, Ipswich Central Boys School (ICBS) with a great teacher, Mr Norman BRYCE for Grade 4 and 5, and with a local Indigenous mate, Vince BUNDA, and others on crowded playgrounds. I was elected Class Monitor. Paul De JERSEY, current Queensland Governor, was also in my 1961 Grade 8 *Scholarship* Class, while his father was Principal. When Darrell completed Junior in 1960— much to my father's objection to 'Sons killing other sons'—Darrell joined the permanent Australian Army with a mate, Ron BELL, as Radio Mechanic Apprentice in cold *Balcombe Barracks*, Victoria, for 9 years, including later serving in the Vietnam War.

My younger brother, Greg, joined me as regular weekday morning

Stories From the Shed

Milk Runner and sharing full days on weekends. We also became initiators/advertisers of Saturday Night Pink *Sports Telegraph* newspaper results—folding, four pence each, collected from keen customers before they had TV coverage (two pence tip to sixpence coin the best earner). These were delivered by loaded push bikes, with Scout and Postie whistles gathering fellow scouts in the dark from homes and lights about frosty 8th Ipswich Cub/Scout Den in Basin Pocket along the east bank of the Bremer River. In 1962–3, I participated with them and others in a long, cold train trip to and from Melbourne for the Pan Pacific/ Australian Scout Jamboree Activities at Dandenong to Anglesea, Victoria. *Quest of the Golden Forest* and other Ventures by Senior Scouts. Later, *Venturers* instilled in me a love of challenges and achievements through camping experiences with others.

I excelled in sprints, broad and long jumps and 'the longer the better' distance races to win two Intermediate Sports Pockets for my school blazer at local and district events. My three sisters attended Ipswich Girls Grammar School and my parents offered to pay for me to attend Ipswich Boys Grammar School, as ISHS was moved from CBD to Brassall. But I said I'd prefer to enrol in a co-educational academic course at Bremer State High School, though ICBS Scholarship results were delayed, so our cohort were placed in class 3A2 until later 4A1. I was promoted to Prefect at Bremer State High School when it was at Silkstone and chastised by the Deputy Principal, Mr. Noel BRADY, for being late to parade—until he realised I'd already done milk-run duties. His family were customers who lived behind us in East Ipswich and later became our neighbours near our first married home when we bought in Pratten St, opposite Corinda State High School.

I switched from soccer to rugby league and was nicknamed

45

Tulloch with my ability to catch a pass from our half-back, as often we had a depleted backline and/or team and I could sprint past defenders to score winning tries. I later played for Booval *Swifts* and the Ipswich under-age representative team in the *Bulimba Cup* against Toowoomba and Brisbane and in conjunction with the main French team game at the North Ipswich Reserve. Though later, Bremer SHS fellow students' cheers at Brisbane RNA/Ekka grounds Championship were suddenly quenched when my final burst of distance racing ended when I became completely exhausted and stumbled before the finish line—what a terrible, humbling feeling. But I'd put my utmost efforts and training into it. I retired early from regular team sports on weekends to concentrate on helping Dad and my family farming pursuits!

When I was only 18, I was elected a Deacon of Rosewood Congregational Church and, by 1974, the Yeronga equivalent, where Rev John RICHARDSON, Secretary of *Qld Congregational Union*, was the Minister who formally confirmed me after my Baptism and that of my first baby daughter, Leanne Fay. This was in the presence of my mother and father, who didn't believe that parents should baptize their children until they were old enough to choose for themselves. Before the *Uniting Church (UC) in Australia* was inaugurated in June, 1977—we'd transferred to Sherwood's Presbyterian Church where they declared me *Life Elder*; but I resigned as *Congregational Leadership Team* member at Oxley Uniting Church later to allow and encourage younger leaders.

I'd earlier been elected President of: *Rosewood Rural Youth Club*, *Rostrum Club 15* at the Land Administration Building and later the *LandCentre*, Woolloongabba, plus the *Weed Society of Qld* as well as instigator of its biennial *Queensland Weeds Symposium* plus later combined *Invasive Pest Animals and Weeds Symposia* rotating around the State; Organiser of Congregational sports days and evening socials; more than 50 Easter *Family Venture* camps; Coordinator of Sherwood and later, Oxley Uniting Church Schools and camps etc. I hitchhiked to *Australasian Association of Ag and Forestry Faculties Student Conferences* in Perth and Hobart. In 1969–70: I led a *Rotary International/ National Union of Australian University Students'* (NUAUS) *National Fitness Camp*; 'Towards Gough WHITLAM's promises for PNG's Self-Government and Independence' for Goroka Teachers College Students and Welfare Officer Women at Mt Hagen State High School, after being the first European to experience living in a local Highlands village for the previous week. After modelling mock parliamentary debates, settling male/female nightly harassments and handing out awards by local dignitaries, I worked at the local butchery, hitchhiked down the notorious Highlands Highway to meet the famous forester pioneer, Romeo LAHEY, and onto Lae. I flew to Port Moresby and sailed out to meet my twin sister, Heather, a missionary teacher and later hospital worker at Iruna United Church of PNG Mission Station, Amazon Bay, half way to Milne Bay.

I met my future wife, Carol Frances BARNETT from Boonah for the first time at a Peak Crossing Hall dance on the Friday evening of my final *B. Agr. Sc. University of Queensland* degree exam, in November, 1970. I then hitchhiked to Sydney, watched *HAIR* at live theatre in Kings Cross before a debrief and boarding a *NUAUS* charter flight to Singapore. After a few days of sightseeing, I and fellow male student shared a Rolls Royce taxi trip to Malacca and on to a previously arranged homestay with a lovely Christian Tamil Family in Kuala Lumpur for Christmas. This turned out to be much more pleasant than the official exchange Indian GP's home further North in Ipoh.

I was invited to accompany a group of young Christians from there by bus to their holiday camp on Penang Island, which was providential. However my scheduled international train trip up the Malay Peninsula to Thailand was blocked by insurgents. So I arranged a visa and caught a ferry to Medan in Indonesian North Sumatra where I had a missionary contact. There was a crowded, rough bus trip down to South Sumatra and a ferry to the bustling capital, Djakarta, of 100,000 betjats (three-wheeler push bike/passenger transporter—cheaper if a customer walked up hills while the betjat contractor pedalled). While travelling overland and visiting *Australian Development Aid Abroad* (ADAB) Ag Projects in Java, I'd learnt some Indonesian communication that helped in Bali rice-growing areas built around contours on steep slopes.

When travelling back through Singapore, I picked up mail from home that informed me that I'd been accepted as an Agronomist in Queensland's *Land Administration Commission* (LAC). So when I finally travelled by train to Bangkok and was offered a seat on a *University of Kuala Lumpur* Students' Coach Trip to Chengmai, I took the opportunity to visit the Hill Tribesmen of the Golden Triangle where Prof NORMAN of Sydney Uni was trying to recruit Ag Scientists to convince them to switch from growing valuable opium to upland rice—but I later left it to a fellow B. Ag. Sc. graduate agronomist, Trevor GIBSON.

Subsequently, from 3rd March 1971, I was employed by the *Land Administration Commission* as one of first three agronomists with Bill CUDDIHY and Tony CALTABIANO, as recommended by the Father of Qld Agriculture, Prof Percy SKERMAN:

1. To examine the economic, agronomic and potential practicalities of development of different sized blocks from vacant Crown coastal lowland/wallum country between Beerwah and Maryborough to Bundaberg and beyond;

2. Seconded to *QDPI's Western Arid Region Land Use Study* (WARLUS) of land systems to drill soil profiles and LANDSAT 3D Mapping S.W. Qld;

3. Expert/agronomist witness to analyse economic position of beef graziers of Lands Dept leasehold land from 1950s when the last beef standard rent was set to present at Land Court hearings throughout the Queensland Land Commissioner's/Agent's Districts.

We sought assistance from relevant sources, visited CSIRO's Beerwah and QDPI's Coolum Research Stations to examine prospects etc.

I completed my B. Econ by External Studies from UQ; but when the 1974 World Beef Price Crash occurred, LAC suspended updating their cattle standard rent for inflation changes etc. In July 1975, I successfully scored Lester PERCY's Weeds Research Agronomist position at LAC's *Alan Fletcher Research Station* (AFRS), Magazine Street, Sherwood.

A.F.R.S. ADVANCING INTEGRATED WEEDS MANAGEMENT

Our team at *Alan Fletcher Research Station* (AFRS) consisted of Entomologists, Plant Pathologists, Agronomists, Chemists, Experimentalists, Sprayers, Trades Technicians, Work Experience/Casuals, Grounds staff, Extension and Clerical Administrators.

Offcuts

They concentrated on researching the biology, life cycle and control options for specific invasive plants, mainly introduced; but they can also be competitive, native problem weeds. This gave AFRS the opportunities to initiate, solve and extend *Integrated Weed Management Programs* (IWMPs) widely by practical demonstrations at Land Managers' Field Days, Council and educational training courses, publications via weed symposia, etc.

The Magazine Street, Sherwood site of the 1860s was Queensland Navy's ammunition stores—upstream Brisbane River from its port, as protection from a Russian threat of invasion. It became Australian Army land from Federation in 1901. The *Commonwealth Prickly Pear Board* chose this site with its heritage house in 1921 as its base and laboratories for quarantining introductions of potential biological control agents of problem prickly pear from the Americas.

This *Cactoblastis cactorum* and other bio-control agents were successfully bred, tested for specificity, multiplied and distributed via various field stations throughout Australia—resulting in managing successive waves of infestations. In 1939, at the start of World War II, rather than have this facility close, the Qld Lands Dept bought it in order to research other problem weeds. From the 1950s, selective herbicides became available to control Noogoora and other burrs in valuable sheep and other pastures that needed research into rates, and integrating manual, mechanical and improved species for competitive pasture management with economical application methods, including aerial agriculture.

In 1967, a new brick office and laboratories building was opened and called *Alan Fletcher Research Station* after the Qld Minister for Lands, with ancillary glass/growth houses that were later extended with controlled climate facilities to simulate conditions suited to imported bio-control agents' origins with appropriate host, test and weedy plants. Further Australian Army land was subsequently bought to extend AFRS to the Brisbane River and Ferry St, on which a large, high-set demountable building was established, along with 'growth tunnels' for propagating water and other weeds for control trials.

AFRS also hosted meetings that led to the formation of the *Weed Society of Qld* in 1975, which inaugurated State weeds forums, and national and international weeds conferences. The first Qld weeds symposium was well supported, even from NSW, at Rockhampton in 1990, next at Townsville in 1992 and Toowoomba in 1994, with subsequent biennial rotations leading to successful, recent invasive pest animals and weeds management symposia, plus useful proceedings for a wider audience.

Thus this dedicated AFRS team has led to efficient, successful *Integrated Weed Management Programs* for Harrisia Cactus, Noogoora Burr, Groundsel Bush, Parthenium Weed, Ambrosia, Rubber Vine, Cats Claw Creeper, Water Weeds and preventing new weeds from establishing before they caused more problems than the cost of containment.

Since AFRS closed in 2010, similar bio-control research has moved to Boggo Road, Dutton Park. It is hoped that the *Dept of Agriculture and Fisheries' Eco-Sciences Precinct* can match these earlier achievements.

Offcuts

VENTURING UP AND DOWN MOUNT BARNEY

Camping adventures have been challenging but worthwhile experiences helping us grow up to mature relationships. From Cub, Boy Scouts to Venturers and other group camps, I progressed to Congregational Church camps at various civilised locations.

However from 1970, I was challenged to risk leaving base camp with bare minimal food, water and camping gear as a Patrol of a few intrepid males plus females to climb the highest mountain in southern Queensland, Mount Barney—just north of the New South Wales Border via the Mt Lindsay Highway, Beaudesert and Barneyview. There was no easy way up or down; but some 'tracks' were easier than others. Even physically disabled Trevor Rees-Thomas was helped up as well as back to Mt. Barney's Saddle via the *Peasants Track* in past years. But climbing East and especially West Peak was much more challenging, requiring clambering up sheer rock faces—even by moonlight.

At Easter 1972 there was no forecast of inclement weather when greeted by a brilliant morning. I led our 3rd Patrol of eight up the Southern Ridge of Mt. Barney, over Razor Back Top to Rum Jungle Camp Site/the *Barney Hut* to cook and share food, drink and Christian Fellowship via three days of Easter devotions plus discussing the un-involvement of many other people. Early the next morning, four of us tried to clamber up West Peak, but only reached half-way when wind and rain became too strong, forcing us back to join others for breakfast.

Our Patrol decided to follow our original, Base Camp logged itinerary down Barney Gorge. Through rain and mist we climbed to high rock formations with slippery detours, around increasing waterfalls via adjacent rain forest, noting native, bluish/colourful crayfish and whip bird calls. We found a dry shelter and lit a fire, boiled water for tea and ate the last of our food rations. All were soaking wet and we were making slow, scary progress. Especially for the girls we were negotiating the safest route via compass and torchlight until the batteries were spent and it was too dark for any of us to proceed.

We experienced the night sleeping in puddles of seeping water under a windy rock overhang. All rose at daybreak to roaring streams over 'Cooees' and 'Hey Bobs' to distant, groups of six fellow campers/potential rescuers; but there were no replies. So we negotiated stream crossings reminiscent of coaxing cattle and calves through tick control plunge dips—as recorded in our Log Book. We left a note at Portals for our searchers and made our own way back to a near-deserted Base Camp, before stopping an official *Search and Rescue* as *Cyclone Emily* warning had scared people home early.

We had never been *lost*; but fasting for 24 hours with similar challenges, brought us closer relationships, with two marriages occurring of two couples involved in our Patrol and still going strong. There were also more, similar introductory meetings and relationships developing, maturing and leading to happy wedded bliss/blessing for other couples after 50 years of *Easter*/now *Uniting Church Family,* but less adventurous camps than this last, most Venture-some Youth camp.

Offcuts

JOHN BROWN

JOHN BROWN HAS an agricultural background, leaving school at the age of fourteen and working on sheep and cattle grazing properties in Victoria and New South Wales before share dairy farming in Queensland. He is widowed after sixty three years of marriage and has three children. He reached senior level by correspondence and became a Stock and Meat Inspector in the Queensland Government. John retired as senior inspector in charge of country slaughterhouses, pet food and butchers' shops in 1987 and has since continued to play an active role in the church and community.

MIDDLE RIDGE

When Ailsa and I moved to Spring Street Toowoomba in 1957 we set about building up the eight-acre farm we had bought. To supplement our income and enable us to pay off the mortgage, we ran fowls, sold eggs, sold milk to the local factory and we grew vegetables selling the surplus to local greengrocers.

Ailsa picked vegetables and dug up the paspalum to make extra garden space near the house. Together we had the little place starting to pay its way when the opportunity to join the Department of Agriculture came my way in 1961.

I was offered a job as cleaner at the car sales building under construction and, from necessity, took it until finding a job at the Darling Downs Bacon factory. It was this position that set me on the way to eventual job satisfaction and fulfilment.

Nearing the completion of the building it was obvious that the painting contractor would not be finished on time for the opening date, only three weeks away so, with two others, I took on a sub-contract which meant working fifteen hours a day.

Rising early I would milk our three cows and then paint until dark, race home for a quick meal and then return and paint under lights until midnight. Ailsa with her two little girls in tow would milk the cows in the evening, feed the pig and lock up the chooks—no mean feat for someone who had never milked a cow before.

One night about eleven o'clock I was on a plank painting a wall when I dozed for a second. Awaking with a start I kicked the plank out from underneath me. I managed to slide down the wall and avoid injury but was not able to prevent the paint from spilling into my hair and over my clothes. Being acrylic paint it washed out and I went home with wet clothes.

We finished the painting on time, using over three hundred gallons of paint. The ceiling consisted of three hundred panels and then we had the cement brick walls as well.

Our neighbours across the road had a poultry farm and I had access to all the fowl manure I needed for growing vegetables and cow feed. I went halves in the cost of a spring-fed dam on their property, and I obtained discarded piping from the Bacon Factory. I bought for five pounds an old dismantled engine, all the parts jumbled in a box.

I managed to get an irrigation system going, using a series of counter shafts to give the underpowered engine enough grunt to pump water to the vegetables and the cow paddocks.

Starting the engine when I came home from work I let it run until ten o'clock, turning it off in the dark, too poor to buy myself a torch. I can hold most electric wires without much trouble and usually test a spark this way but the magneto on my engine was the best I have experienced. More than once I was zapped when groping for the stop switch in the dark. The zap was so severe it would sting far worse than the electric shock.

I saw an advertisement in the local newspaper: 'Twelve horsepower Howard rotary hoe for sale' and, with my interest aroused, I appeared at the address given, with a view to purchasing the thing for one hundred and twenty pounds. Some haggling with the woman saw me buy it for eighty pounds. I loaded it onto the back of my Commer utility. I set off for home with the front wheels barely touching the road.

After much care and attention a crop of peas matured that we had planted in partnership with two friends from work. With our wives we picked and sold them, each family making thirty pounds for their efforts. I went to the shed to start my rotary hoe to cultivate the pea paddock only to find a thief had stolen my Rotary Hoe magneto. A new one cost me twenty-eight pounds which meant that I only made two pounds from my pea-growing enterprise and three months effort. I used the pea stalks for cow feed and the peas would have put some nitrogen into the soil.

Not realising that the magneto timing was timed from the front piston when fitting my replacement, I set the V engine incorrectly with the result that, when starting, it was correct on one piston but not on the other. Starting was by crank handle at the side. I preferred to use the handle like the foot pedal start of a motor bike, which was easier than swinging on the handle in normal circumstances. As I kicked down, my foot slipped off and behind the handle just as the motor backfired causing the handle to hit me on the calf half-way up my leg. Ailsa's friend from next door came racing across the road to tell her: 'John is over in the paddock rolling in the dirt!' Again all I got out of the incident was loss of pride and severe bruising and I can't remember whether sympathy or a lecture from my wife.

A crop of tomatoes ripened at the time when they were at their dearest and we received three pounds five a case for two cases before getting a severe hailstorm wiping out the entire crop. That same storm came just on sunset and the hail was so severe that it blocked the roof gullies, causing the water to dam up and overflow in through the ceiling. I had to go out in the raging storm, climb onto the roof and shovel the hail off in the midst of the tempest. Several months later a hailstorm wiped out our vegetables and stippled our cow feed to the ground.

I was working at the bacon factory in late 1958 when I heard there was to be an entrance examination for recruitment of stock and meat inspectors. Study could be done by correspondence. Though I had little education to that point in my life I felt that I could succeed, the only drawback being that the others had been studying for many months. I was considering study as the positions offered secure employment and retirement pension benefits greater than the old age pension. Ailsa immediately said, 'I am sure you could do it.' Her encouragement was enough for me, and out of overtime money we scraped up the fifteen pounds to pay for the correspondence course.

I would milk in the morning and deliver the milk to the factory on the way to work and, if I was called on to do overtime, Ailsa would milk the cows. I worked the farm at weekends and we grew vegetables to sell to a greengrocer in town as well as some to regular customers. Each fortnight I would put in two rows of beans and if the price wasn't right I would feed them to the cows. Watering at night while I studied was no problem. Ailsa picked most of the beans and also produced a fine son.

I confined my correspondence studies to an hour a night, with some reminder notes in my pocket to check, and I would spend the lunch break revising. The night hour study was after the kids had gone to bed and, for this time, I shut everything out. This allowed me to get in my sleep as well as keep the farm in order.

We were always short of cow food, so we needed to supplement by collecting from the side of the road. Usually we took a utility load of clover or rye grass home after a visit to Ailsa's father for Sunday lunch. To use a scythe well is a skill that only comes from regular use and no patch of clover or rye grass escaped my attention as I collected my weekly treat for the cows.

I passed my exams and now it was a matter of waiting for a vacancy. That vacancy came in an offer to become an Inspector of Stock at Bundaberg in 1961.

A new chapter in our lives was beginning and, in Bundaberg, it was a perfect springboard to a life of fulfilment and a full life to follow in retirement.

PASSING IT ON

For more than twenty years an annual street party festival has been held, with the local shopping centre street at Sherwood being closed for several hours on a Friday night in November each year. I served on the organising committee for twelve years until I was no longer covered by insurance. I was not prepared to lose my house should anyone on the committee make a wrong choice. Still, I have continued to serve as a volunteer mainly with preparations on the night and organising signage prior to the festival. Ailsa and I were active with the running of the Church stalls at the festival.

One of my special annual events is the yearly reunion of past and present members of the DPI where I have a chance to catch up with colleagues—many of whom I had coached for the DPI entrance exams and who I had on my team as butcher's shop inspectors when I retired. It has been very pleasing to meet up with these men and learn of their efforts to go even further in enriching their lives by finding rewarding jobs and careers. Most of them had been meat workers or butchers working on wages.

I played a significant role in organising the *National Anglican Men's Society Council* one hundredth anniversary celebrations held in Brisbane in 2005 and the AMS National Meeting in Brisbane in 2010—in the first instance as treasurer and in the second as Queensland Chairman, a position I occupied for four years. My time as Queensland Chairman was most rewarding, as was all my service with the AMS over the past fifty-four years.

At the 2010 meeting in Brisbane National Chairman Bishop Richard Hurford and several invited speakers urged us to go out of our comfort zone and reach out to people. Bishop Hurford threw out the challenge in words that sounded to me like: 'Go out there and do something about it if you want to be an organisation with a purpose.' I had always felt a passion for doing something about it but thought I didn't have the ability to do it until the Holy Spirit showed me the way.

St John's Church forms part of the Anglican Parish of Sherwood and, as Sub-Warden at St John's, I took up the Bishop's challenge and sought the approval of the Parish Council to investigate the possibility of setting up a *Men's Shed* under the Oxley Church Hall. This area had seen little use, and I felt the space would be ideal for a *Men's Shed*. I sought the approval of my Rector who was most supportive and encouraged me to call a meeting to gauge the interest.

At a meeting set up by the local Brisbane City Council member, strong support from the meeting encouraged me to form a Steering Committee, and from that proceed to form the *St John's Oxley Community Men's Shed.* With Sherwood Parish Council and Diocesan approval the project could now go ahead. A Brisbane City Council grant application was successful, resulting in the construction of a lock-up section for the safe storage of necessary shed equipment; stage one of our journey.

There was a long road ahead for us including further building approvals etc. to enclose the work area, and from donations and grants we were able to build our shed and get necessary equipment—forty years on since the hall was raised.

In 1948 I rode a motor bike from Ashford to Coleraine, Victoria, and on a lonely stretch of road blew a tyre. A well-dressed man in his flash car saw my plight and took me to his workshop behind his grand homestead. Sensing that I was hungry he insisted on me having a meal at the station cookhouse and, when I had finished, there sitting outside was my bike ready to go, with the original tyre perfectly restored with a vulcanized patch. His workmen had retrieved and repaired my bike while I ate. He drove up in his car, had a brief chat and apologised because he had to leave to go to a meeting.

Full of gratitude I asked him if I could pay him and received an answer that in no small way has influenced many of my decisions since. 'God gave me the opportunity to help. When you get the chance just pass it on.' I have often had the chance and hope to get more to keep his mustard tree growing. I continued my journey, pointing my boots in the direction I was heading, and promptly went to sleep under my ground sheet, sleeping until first light. My passion is to pass it on until I pass on, and one of the best places is *Men's Shed*.

RETIREMENT

Having been blessed with a life so full of adventure and reward, we were ready now to put behind us the bug to travel overseas and instead concentrate on home life and occasional bus tours in Australia and an occasional short break by car to places we had not yet been. My family in Victoria and Ailsa's in Toowoomba were getting older and we frequently spent time in short visits to see them, often combining these trips with the opportunity to catch up with people we had befriended in our life journey.

I continued my active role in the *Anglican Men's Society* and represented the Society as a delegate to the *National Council* annual meetings in Queensland, New South Wales, Victoria, Western Australia and Tasmania, taking the opportunity to make new friends and catch up with old ones as well as take in the local tourist places and scenery. On our overseas trip to Europe in 1987 we befriended two couples from Western Australia and on one of our AMS Meeting trips to Perth we took time to stay there for a chance to meet with them. They in turn had visited us and we recalled the pleasant trip we had in thirty days through thirteen countries in Europe.

Not long after my retirement I was one of the Sherwood Parish Wardens for several years and realised that the church and hall at St John's Oxley were getting a little tired both inside and out and needed brightening up. We engaged a painter to paint the interior of the church at St John's and each week I would shuffle the pews around to allow the painter to paint and, of a Sunday, have them ready for the service. The porch entrance was not included in this exercise and I later did this painting of the walls and metal roof as well as rearranging the display boards.

The altar at St John's was so positioned that the Priest had his back to the people for the communion and it was accepted by Church Council that I could extend the sanctuary platform to enable the Altar to be reversed. I consider this was my best carpentry effort ever, or as good as my effort with the house at Laidley. I was pleased with my efforts until I was told that council approval wasn't the only approval necessary; I should have had Diocesan approval as well. The delayed approval was forthcoming after my apologies as well as those of the Rector and the paperwork submitted.

When we sold our property at Laidley, I now had plenty of time to do hobby work and gardening as well as church work both at St Matthew's in Sherwood and St John's in Oxley, and also in painting of the hall roof with the help of others at Sherwood. It was a different story at Oxley where I could only muster one helper and, while he did a good job in painting the windows and trims, he was unable to paint the walls because of shoulder problems. Over a period of six months, I painted the exterior of both the church and the hall using only ladders and planks and then spent eight weeks painting the ceilings and interior walls of the hall. In all, with the washing and sanding down, the exercise took four manoeuvres of trestles and planks several times each day.

Many times I was painting alone but Ailsa insisted that when I was using the high ladders I should wait until my trim man was there to keep an eye on me; which I mostly did. My man Ken had a bad shoulder and couldn't do the heavy work and therefore was not always there. One morning I suggested to Ailsa that I would await Ken's arrival before touching up a missed section of the hall outer walls. But Ken was held up and I did the job alone. As I stepped down off the ladder after completing the task I saw Ailsa coming around the corner bringing me morning tea. I felt like a school kid caught playing the wag.

The wooden crosses on the church, four in all, had rotted away and were hanging loosely, with rainwater entering the space in the metal roof causing rotting in the rafters. My nephew Glen made up metal crosses with a saddle that I could bolt to the roof using silicone to seal it so that it would be waterproof. To put them in place I had an extendable ladder and, for three of them, I could without much risk or difficulty get them affixed. However, for the last one it was difficult because the position of the porch made it impossible to reach from the ladder. It meant that I either had to slide along the ridge for the full length of the church with a bucket full of tools or resort to a better plan.

Tying a series of ropes from one side of the church to the other I was able to place a ladder on the guttering and reach the ridge and complete the anchorage of the last cross. To get down was a problem. I called down to Ken to move the ladder to the right and he attempted to do just that, but his bad shoulder caused him to lose control, with the ladder crashing to the ground. I was stranded on the ridge. It was no good me trying to slide along the ridge as I still would need a ladder, so I threw the bucket of tools down. Then I made my scary way down hand-over-hand on the rope, relieved and thanking God for keeping me safe.

The ladder looked okay and I took it home to take care of a few neglected jobs, deciding to paint the fascia at the end wall of our high-set home. Ailsa had a beautiful geranium garden along the side boundary, and rather than stand the ladder on this, I had it on too much of a slant and apparently the ladder had been damaged in the fall at the church. Suddenly with a paint tin in one hand and a paint brush in the other and fifteen feet up the wall I heard a cracking and saw the upper part of the ladder splintering. With no time to lose I tossed the paint and brush aside and leapt, missing the splinters but not the bottom rung, which tumbled me at speed into the geranium bed. I think the poem I wrote while in agony, recovering from the incident, tells the story. I still claim I have never fallen off a ladder.

Offcuts

Bill Barker

WILLIAM BARKER, THE THIRD ELDEST of nine brothers and one sister, grew up in Brisbane. He was conscripted for compulsory National Service in 1966, eventually serving from 1968 for two years in the Royal Australian Army Service Corps. One year was served at Nui Dat, Vietnam, from May 1969 to May 1970. He was a primary school teacher and principal; married Mary in 1973. He has a daughter and three sons, thirteen grandchildren and one great-grandson. On retirement, he continued wood-turning and took up traditional rocking horse carving. His stories are for his children and grandchildren.

DEPARTURE

It's 13 May 1969, a cool spring evening in Sydney.

Dressed in my summer Army uniform, I am standing alone in a very large, crowded hangar at Mascot Airport, Sydney. There are no frills of a departure lounge, just a large open space. Hundreds of people of all ages are here, including about two hundred military personnel in summer dress of varying colours.

I walk slowly around the hangar, looking for a familiar face.

There is a gentle hum of voices, softly echoing throughout the huge building as people cluster in pairs or small family groups, talking quietly, just standing, hugging, being together. Children stand close to their parents, bewildered as to what is happening.

There are tears and the occasional sob as the midnight departure time draws near.

I had left Brisbane for Sydney after a week's pre-embarkment leave, which had been preceded by a two-week jungle warfare training course at Canungra. My only training as a fighting soldier.

As I was departing Brisbane, my mother had indicated that my eldest brother, Anthony, would be in Sydney to farewell me on behalf of the family. Being taller than most people, I'm able to view a large part of the hangar. But to no avail; somewhat disappointed, I could not find my brother. All I see are the clusters of people as they say their good-byes; I feel their soft, tender tension.

The last week before departure I had spent stationed at Sydney's South Head, Watson's Bay Transit Centre, waiting with nothing much to do. I knew no one else there. They, like me, were just waiting. Each day, I left the transit centre and wandered Sydney alone.

On one of my meanderings, I saw St Mary's Cathedral. I entered and found a sense of peace and quiet. I sat in that tranquil space, trying to come to terms with what the next twelve months would bring. What was going to war all about—and, in particular, a war in which friend and foe can be one and the same?

The uncertainty and the unknown make me restless and apprehensive, coupled with the knowledge that I can do nothing about it. I realise that once on the plane with my fellow re-enforcements, I will be at war by lunch tomorrow, 14 May 1969, a Wednesday, and will be in Vietnam for the next 366 days.

There is no announcement to board. We just seem to know that it's time. With no one to say good-bye to, I join the quiet procession to the plane. I go through a large exit and across the dimly lit tarmac to the steps of the plane. I climb the stairs of the Qantas 707, knowing that there are two stopovers, Darwin, and Singapore, before I reach Saigon.

I check to see that I have my civilian shirt with me for our stop-over in Singapore. Because Singapore is a neutral country, we're required to wear the shirt while we have breakfast in the terminal waiting for the clearance to fly on into Saigon's Tan Son Nhut Airport.

No one speaks, except for a voice that calls for me to keep a seat near me. It's John Cahill, a warrant officer, WO1, with ASCU, my unit, whom I had met at Canungra for the first time. The plane is at capacity with a total male crew and no seating distinction for rank. I am sitting with John Cahill and a Catholic chaplain.

The flight is less than memorable. We chat for a while and then try to sleep. I am given a can of beer before we land in Darwin. We are told to remain on the plane in Darwin. I'm led to believe that we are taking on extra fuel, sufficient fuel for the return flight to Darwin if we cannot land in Saigon. There is another can of beer on the flight to Singapore, where we are off-loaded for breakfast, into an empty terminal. I am wearing my civilian shirt.

The landing in Saigon goes without a hitch; but as the doors of the plane open, the noise of war and the extreme humidity flood in on us. The noise and the humidity envelop us as we wait in the middle of the tarmac for orders. As we collect our kit bags, the sounds of fighter jets, transports and helicopters fill the air. I know we are at war.

As I stand there, waiting for orders, I hope that, in 12 months' time, I will be standing on this same spot, but going the opposite way, going home.

Offcuts

THE TOILET BLOCK

Vung Tau, a port on the south of South Vietnam's east coast, was the supply port for the Australian Task Force during the Vietnam War. It was a busy port town, a fishing village, much like any port anywhere in the world, except it was supplying Australian troops with equipment, food and weapons for a war just beyond the town's borders.

It was a peaceful place, probably for both sides—the Australians and the Viet Cong. In the middle of the town, the Australian forces had an R & C Centre (Rest and Convalescence), where soldiers could take a short break when needed. Both forces seemed to rest together.

My unit, 2 Australian Forces Canteen Unit, a unit within the Royal Australian Army Services Corps (RAASC), was situated close to the main entrance to the Vung Tau Base. The platoon commander, Major Keith Frampton, had his headquarters within the Vung Tau Base. Each day, when he was at work, the ASCU flag would fly from the unit's flag-pole outside his office.

Every few months the supply ship, *HMAS Jeparit*, with escorts, would arrive in Vung Tau with a full cargo of ammunition, civil aid program stores and supplies, vehicles (including tanks), food and supplies for the entire Task Force and stocks for the Australian Services Canteen Unit. The deadline was three days to unload and transport the cargo to destinations throughout the Vung Tau base, and unload and store in neat, designated locations for easy distribution later—three days of twelve-hour shifts.

As 2IC of Nui Dat's Bulk Store, one of my many skills was forklift driver. To do the unloading and loading of pallets and small containers, I had a grey-green Massey Ferguson tractor.

Once the *Jeparit's* date and time of arrival were known, I was ordered to go to Vung Tau to help unload the trucks that came from the wharf. We had three long, hot dusty days—the long hot days of the dry season—to complete the task.

At first light on day one, I collected a Case forklift from the transport depot, a huge machine compared to my Massey Ferguson that I operated at Nui Dat, but still quite manageable. I had driven similar machines at The Dat, unloading ammunition when a driver was needed, but this one was a little different, seemed to break in the middle as it turned. The complete cabin turned with the forks.

By the end of day one, we were exhausted, sweaty, and completely covered in bulldust. For two-and-a-half days we worked tirelessly, unloading trucks that arrived in a seemingly endless stream.

The work was repetitive and mundane, container after container, pallet after pallet being stacked three or four high into an ever-decreasing space within the compound. Each pile was covered by tarpaulins lifted onto the stacks by the fork-lifts and manually spread by the other members of the platoon working in the compound. Over these days, there was the sameness, the hum of three fork-lifts working constantly with the trucks lining up to be unloaded in the heat and the bulldust. It was constant and monotonous.

The third day started just as the other two, at first light. I remember clearly that the trucks were now bringing loads of Carlton beer, enough beer for over 5000 soldiers for three months, and sensed that storage space was becoming limited.

Late in the afternoon, I was directed by the Warrant Officer, 'Macca' McInnes, to start filling the narrow area between the boundary fence and the large store shed. This was to give the beer that did not fit in the sheds some little extra protection while under the tarps. Only one machine would fit; so, it became my job alone. I had to carefully squeeze around the corner of the bulk store and a toilet block, then between the shed and the

side security fence. It was a small, tight area to work in, going in forward and then reversing all the way out to near the trucks, and then grabbing another pallet off the truck and repeating the process over and over.

The afternoon wore on repetitively, one pallet at a time stacked neatly behind the shed—necessary, but boring work. I was hot, covered in fine bulldust and looking forward to the last truckload that was becoming increasingly near at hand. I decided to make a slight difference, a small non-consequential change to add variety, to break the routine, to have a little adaption. I decided to reverse part of the way out from the stack of pallets and to then turn slightly towards the toilet block, also along the boundary fence, and go forward towards the waiting truck—not much of a variation, but different.

My first and only attempt at a change was memorable. I did the reverse as usual, but I added the slight turn towards the fence-line building, the toilet block. As I turned, I noticed the other two fork-lifts working on the other side of the compound and did not take too much interest as to what I was doing. I knew that I had plenty of room to turn.

My sense of achievement and satisfaction was to be short-lived. Much to my complete surprise, I heard a loud splintering crash of wood; but that could not be—I was too far from the building. I was surprised yet not overly concerned at the sounds of splintering wood; somewhat puzzled, but not enough to stop and look. I was too tired to fully come to terms with what had just happened. I went forward again and became wedged close to the Bulk Store. So, I reversed again, only to have the sounds of destruction repeated.

Offcuts

This time I stopped and looked down behind me. I was somewhat surprised to see an angry, pale-faced Major, my boss, emerge, clambering over a crushed toilet door while pulling up his trousers. There was movement from all the other diggers working in the compound on hearing the toilet doors being demolished.

Major Eric Frampton bellowed at me to get off my machine and to stand at attention beside my fork-lift. Dressed in hat, shorts and boots, I dutifully complied, quite apprehensive as to what the major might do. A large crowd had gathered at a safe distance from the major, but in full view of what might be about to happen.

I was expectant as I pondered what Major Frampton was thinking and what lay ahead, but also silently admiring the precise piece of demolition, I had just accomplished. My fork-lift's large tow bar, which I had forgotten about, had gone neatly through his toilet door while he was sitting on the 'throne'. There was no other damage to the toilet block building except the two doors, two out of eight and two toilets apart.

There is always a saving angel. At the very moment Major Frampton was about to give me the best dressing down and probably a charge of endangering the life of an officer, the second demolished toilet door crumbled to the ground.

There, framed in the doorway, was a middle-aged Vietnamese female cleaner, shaking appreciably and quite pale as she clambered over the wreckage and disappeared swiftly into the distance.

The assembled crowd burst into the loudest, raucous, and most welcomed laughter that I have ever heard. Even the WO1, Macca McInnis, could not restrain himself from joining the gales of laughter from the assembling crowd. Of the eight toilets, I had selected the only two that were occupied.

Major Frampton stood dumbfounded and silent, while the crowd enjoyed the moment.

His next words were calmer than I had expected. He told me to go and collect my gear and be ready to take the late flight back to Nui Dat. The unloading was almost complete, and I was not needed any more. However, in the next few days I would be needed to unload the trucks at Nui Dat.

I was not charged and nor did I lose my corporal stripes. To this day, I still wonder what they both thought as the tow bar came through the toilet door.

THE FLAG

As you might well know, all military units have a flag that they will defend to the ultimate, to death, if required. My unit was no different, so I thought—Det. 2 Platoon, Australian Forces Canteen Unit (AFCU).

We, at Nui Dat, the Sharp End, were a small unit comprising a second lieutenant, two warrant officers, and a corporal and three diggers. We latter four lived in a sandbagged four-man tent with pallets as flooring, in among the rubber trees. We were in a section of the Task Force that was designated the Task Force Maintenance Area (TFMA)—an area that accommodated all the small odd-bod units such as postal, fuel, pay, drivers and many more. Most of these sub-units were part of Royal Australian Army Service Corps.

Previously, our Nui Dat contingent had noted that our lieutenant, Colin Ward, did not have a flag or even a flag pole at his office, at the end of the PX at Nui Dat. The general feeling was that we, too, should have had an AFCU flag flying at Nui Dat. But that was never to be.

The Australian Forces Canteen Unit flag proudly flew at Vung Tau, from where our Nui Dat platoon was administered by the aforementioned officer, Major Keith Frampton. Outside his administration building stood the flag pole on which the AFCU flag was raised each morning and lowered at sunset.

This story comes about on one evening about half-way through my tour of duty. I'm in Vung Tau for a unit briefing and an evening social gathering of the whole platoon—all twenty of us.

Drinks are easily obtained, but we did do a trade for the BBQ ingredients. The celebration is held in the AFCU compound recreational area, which is in the Vung Tau Task Force Area's secured zone. It's a good night of eating, drinking, chatting, even story-telling and attempts at singing. It's an evening to take our minds off where we are and why we are here. However, there's always a time when you realise that, throughout life, one must take and hold opportunities as they present themselves. They might never come again.

Towards the latter part of the evening, I'm having a long and deep conversation with the warrant officer WO1 'Macca' Phil McInnis, from Vung Tau, a nice bloke. He's trying to convince me, a National Serviceman, of the merits of becoming a regular soldier and how an officer's role could present itself if I ever decided to sign on.

As the evening progressed towards midnight, others started to drift off to the accommodation huts up among the sand hills throughout the base. Macca and I clean up. He goes off to lock up and check if the security has arrived for the night. I start to wander back to the lines where I am staying. The soldiers here have huts with an attached shower room.

As I walk towards the front gate of the AFCU compound, I pass the flag-pole and notice that the flag is still flying. It has not been taken down at sunset. Being a good and loyal soldier, I decide to take down the flag because that is the right thing to do. I'm careful, in my light-headed state, not to let the flag touch the ground.

I carefully fold the flag as small as I can, but I can't find anywhere safe and secure to store it. I can't see Macca anywhere or any open doors. Thinking very clearly, in my light headed state I decide that the safest thing to do is to take it with me back to the lines and place it in my kit bag for safe keeping. It will be safe there until the next morning.

At first light, I am up early to tidy my sleeping area, as a good soldier should, and because I must be at the airstrip ready to fly back to Nui Dat to begin work at the normal time. There's still no safe place to leave the flag. I don't trust the diggers who work at the AFCU compound at Vung Tau; so, I just leave it in my kit bag and fly back to Nui Dat.

I'm surprised that there's not any consternation from Vung Tau— no discussion from the authorities as to the whereabouts of the missing flag. No one seems to be noticing the flag's absence. I'm quite prepared to own up to its whereabouts and where it might be found. But no one seems concerned; so neither was I. And the flag stayed in my metal trunk under my bed.

It is only towards the end of my tour I learn that fortune does favour the brave.

It came to my notice that very next morning, after the party, that the old flag was due to be replaced with a new one that had just been sent from Australia. The soldier whose duty it was to raise the flag that morning, took the new flag and raised it with no knowledge that the old flag had simply disappeared.

Postscript: In September 2019, I offered the flag, with the story, to the Australian War Memorial, which, in response, told me to keep it safe.

Stories From the Shed

James Vernon

James Vernon had a variety of interests and occupations before his retirement. He trained to be a French horn player; had his own photographic studio; studied to be a high school teacher and finally became a teacher of English to speakers of other languages and examiner for the *International English Language Testing System*. These occupations were interspersed with two periods of boredom in the public service. Now he is retired and spends his days reading, writing and pursuing his interest in photography. The advent of Covid-19 caused him to make a website to show his photography, (www.jamesvernonphotography.com). Life is good.

A PRIVILEGED CHILDHOOD

We took over the boarding house at 23 Adsett St Taringa when I was in year five, aged 10, I think. It was a big change. We went from a small house on the flat at Chelmer to a huge house on a quite steep hill at Taringa. (If I remember correctly it had seven bedrooms and two 'sleepouts'.) Instead of living as a nuclear family we shared the place with up six or seven other people. I not only had my own room, one of the 'sleepouts', but I had to travel by train to school every day. These two aspects gave me plenty of time alone. The latter gave me the opportunity to supplement my income as a 'stringer', collecting sports results for the Saturday evening edition of the *Telegraph* newspaper, by travelling without a ticket to school.

We had purchased the boarding house from the son of a friend of Mum's as a business venture. He and his wife appeared to have operated it quite successfully. Mum, being the woman she was, soon made it a house of friends—not a good way to operate such an enterprise.

Dad had aspirations to extend the house by building two flats underneath it. I remember him poring over blueprints that he had drawn himself in the lounge room. His planned extension had to be done economically. To this end he had a load of uncleaned, second-hand bricks delivered. The old mortar had to be removed before they could be used. Being soft and easily powdered, removing the mortar wasn't too bad. However, a substantial percentage of them had been faced with cement on one or two sides. Removing this was murder. I remember spending several days during Christmas holidays engaged on this task with leather gloves and a tomahawk. The gloves got holes in them first and then my hands. On one memorable occasion I cleaned over a hundred bricks in a day. Sadly, the flats were started but never completed.

At the weekends we frequently shared the dining room with the boarders. The time between the meal and the washing-up was usually spent in lively discussion or playing cards. The rule for the discussions was simple—talk about anything you like except Politics, Sex or Religion. As a result of these discussions my education was supplemented by hearing about a wide range of topics. I first heard the names of the greats of western philosophy during a dining-room debate between a philosophy student and blue-singleted labourer. It seemed to me the 'uneducated' worker more than held his own. He certainly seemed to have equal facility in citing the experts.

The boarders were a motley group. It was mainly male and working class. The previous owners had recommended being a fully male establishment, as women in a boarding house cause TROUBLE. This recommendation was made despite the fact that they had a token female boarder themselves when we took over. However, she kept her own counsel and we really only saw her at meal times. We frequently had one or two students from the University of Queensland. There was also a member of what would now be referred to as the IT department at the university. He regularly brought home large metal frames, about 50x60 centimetres, on which he soldered intricate patterns in fine wire. He assured me that this was done to program the computer. Now you know where we would be without transistors and the like.

MARGARITA

Mum did make some exceptions to the 'no women' policy. The first of these was Margarita.

Margarita was Latvian. I suspect she migrated to Australia to escape the chaos of post-war Europe. She had some characteristics that should have endeared her to a masculine establishment—she was young and quite attractive. For some reason she didn't quite fit in. She spoke excellent English but with the precision of grammar and pronunciation that one finds only in a fluent non-native speaker.

She was well-educated and was studying at the university. She might have even been working there. She enjoyed classical music. Mozart symphonies and the like were frequently heard emanating from the radio in the lounge room if she got there first. (This was to my dismay as I was into Rock'n'Roll at the time.) Above all, to use an old-fashioned term, Margarita was 'ladylike'.

It might have been that while she had mastered the language, she hadn't come to terms with working-class Australian culture. I suppose you could say that her relationships in the house were reservedly friendly, at least for a while. True, she was the butt of good-natured working-class banter at times, although she never really seemed to see the joke and so she wasn't offended.

One night, Dad mentioned a humorous poem that one of his workmates at the Ipswich Railway Workshops claimed to have written. Naturally he was prevailed upon to read it to the assembly. (I suspect that his friend's claim to literary fame was spurious. I recently Googled the first line to refresh my memory of it and found it on several different websites. One of these is given here with some alterations to incorporate bits from my memory.)

Dad launched into it with relish, but I've quoted only some of the verses here in the interests of brevity:

> 'A farmer's dog once came to town
> His Christian name was Pete.
> His pedigree was ten yards long
> His looks were hard to beat.
>
> He never missed a landmark,
> He never missed a post,
> For piddling was his masterpiece
> And piddling was his boast.'

Margarita looked bemused.

OFFCUTS

'The city dogs stood looking on
In deep and jealous rage
To see this little country dog
The piddler of the age.

They sniffed him over one by one
They sniffed him two by two
But noble Pete in high disdain
Stood still 'til they were through.

When they'd smelt him everywhere
Their praise for him ran high
But when one sniffed him underneath
Pete piddled in his eye.'

Margarita looked puzzled. She looked even more confused as Dad continued on with a string of verses on the same theme, including:

'Then all the dogs from far and wide
Were summoned with a yell.
They'd hold a piddling carnival
And judge him by his smell.

They showed him all the piddling posts
They knew about the town
And off they set with many a wink
To wear the stranger down.

But Pete was with them all the way
With vigour and with vim

> A thousand piddles more or less
> Were all the same to him.
>
> And on and on went noble Pete
> As tireless as a windmill
> And very soon those city dogs
> Were piddled to a standstill.'

Margarita seemed to be becoming aware that she was receiving amused, sidelong glances as Dad finished off the poem:

> 'The city dogs said "farewell Pete,
> Your piddling did defeat us,"
> But no one ever put them wise
> That Pete... had diabetes.'

Margarita was nonplussed. 'Please, what is piddling?'

One of the boarders enlightened her in basic language that left no doubt about the meaning.

Margarita looked affronted. With a sudden intake of air, she stood bolt-upright, knocking her chair backwards with a bang, and exited stage left in high dudgeon.

The room was momentarily silent. This was followed by sideways looks and some suppressed chuckles as the embarrassing humour of the situation sank in.

The poetry reading soon receded into the background, as such incidents do, and polite decorum was restored. That is, until the night when Margarita excused herself from the table a little earlier than usual on the grounds that she had to work on a university assignment.

'What's it about'?

'Class distinction in Australia,' came the innocent reply.

Gasp! This was heresy! Every man and his dog knew that class distinction in this country had been consigned to the dustbin of history! Australians didn't kowtow to anyone! Jack was as good as his master! True, the Workingman's Paradise hadn't quite been achieved—yet. But give us time. Naturally, this provoked a lively, not particularly academic debate until Margarita decided that work called her elsewhere.

She wasn't exactly ostracised but she was regarded with a rather formal but cordial politeness by some of the boarders. Not long after this Margarita moved out. It seems that she had a boyfriend somewhere and wanted to be closer to him.

One night one of the boarders returned home with a *Telegraph* newspaper and a solemn look on his face.

'Have you seen the paper?' he enquired. 'Margarita's dead. She was killed in a car accident.'

The house was very subdued for a while after that.

BILL, GORDON AND NED

The boarding house was a repository for some real characters. One of these was Old Bill. He was a wiry, sunbrowned bushy who drank, smoked and consorted with women 'of a certain kind'. Mum always reckoned he was a 'diamond in the rough'. He tried to give me advice about life.

On one Saturday he came home from the races in a very alcoholically enhanced mood, that is, not safe to drive but certainly not offensive or obnoxious. He drew me aside and lowered his voice to a conspiratorial level.

'I won't be home tonight,' he confided. 'Goin' to the wrestlin'. Yer a bit young yet for this advice. But when yer older and want a woman, go ter the wrestlin' or the boxin'. Yer'll get a woman for sure! They go crazy afterwards!' He didn't come home that night. On a couple of occasions he'd wink at me and whisper, 'Boxin' tonight. See ya after Mass tomorrer!' I guess Old Bill was quite religious in his own way.

While Bill's advice in matters of the flesh was amusing, his guidance in the art of poker was much more useful to a celibate prepubescent.

Bill had a mate. Together they were a really odd couple. While Bill was probably in his fifties, Gordon was at least twenty years younger. Bill was a bushy; Gordon was urbane. Bill and I got on well; Gordon disliked me intensely. I had beaten him at chess, drafts and canasta. I liked to think that I had also beaten him in a fight but it's more likely that the certainty of eviction caused him to beat a strategic withdrawal from the conflict.

So, when we faced off against each other over the table on one of the frequent 'penny poker' nights, things were bound to get interesting.

The game proceeded with its usual small change bets (also known as 'shrapnel'), and the usual good-natured banter. Then the mood slowly changed. I picked up my hand and looked. Depending on what replaced the discards, three cards could combine for either a flush or a straight. I kept those and received the replacements which gave me both a flush and a straight with the pictures. This had to be a good hand!

The bids started. The pot grew while the participants dwindled. Eventually it was just Gordon and me left. I was not going to quit as my stake dwindled. I borrowed from practically everyone in the game. Mum was 'having kittens', to use Dad's description. Gordon was sure I was bluffing as I frequently did. Bill stole a look at my hand and I sensed a sudden intake of air. 'Don't throw it in,' he whispered. 'I'll stake you for whatever you need.' Gordon faltered and paid to see my hand.

Slowly and deliberately I put out the cards without taking my eyes off Gordon. 'Ten, jack, queen, king, ace. All hearts.' Gordon paled and nearly choked on his anger as I raked in my winnings. I won about a week's wages for an adult that night. 'That was a royal flush. It's the unbeatable hand,' gasped Bill. 'I've been playing poker all my life and never seen one.' I'm not sure if Gordon ever forgave Bill for his treachery. There certainly seemed to be a bit of distance between them for a while.

I think Mum suggested substituting matches for coins after that and the games became less frequent. Matches just didn't have the same feeling. As for me, I don't think I've played poker since. Well, once you've hit the top there doesn't seem to be much point.

The boarders were a disparate bunch. Virtually all were male and unmarried. A couple were separated or divorced and one or two were engaged. A couple had girlfriends that we never saw. Looking back I would guess that a number (probably about ten per cent) were gay, but at that time it was very much a matter of 'Don't ask, don't tell'.

The boarding house was an interesting and stimulating environment for a kid. Apart from the salacious advice of old

Bill, there were a number who passed on real education. Ned Chandler was one of these. He had served in the Middle East during the Second World War. He was a shop assistant, ('counter jumper', according to Dad), at one of the classy jewellers in the city. Ned might not have had much formal education but he had the most encyclopaedic knowledge of anyone that I have met and was very willing to pass it onto me. In the course of his occupancy he showed me the eye of a moth with his pocket microscope, taught me how to develop a roll of film and make a contact print as well as explaining the working of an aneroid barometer. On one occasion he saw me reading a biography of Leonardo Da Vinci. This prompted a spontaneous, hour-long tutorial on the Renaissance.

When he left he entrusted a set of illustrated books on Australian actions in the Second World War to me saying that he would come back and get them 'sometime'. Time passed and it started to look as if I had inherited them. One day a car with a woman and a couple of teenagers pulled up outside and Ned got out and came to the house. We hadn't known that he was married when he was a boarder. He might have hidden this knowledge because of the general opprobrium attached to men who 'deserted' their families. Of course, to me, the significance of his return was that I had to surrender his books.

MOLLY

Then Mum realised that there was a widow, Molly, living by herself next door at number 25. We would see her arriving home sometimes, usually a bit unsteady on her feet and with a number of bottles under her arms. Rumour had it that she had been a concert pianist and had gone to pieces after her husband died. I don't know how true that was. She certainly had a nice looking piano in the lounge room but I never heard her play it.

So, Mum being Mum, she invited Molly for dinner occasionally. The first few times went without incident. But then came the 'Night of the Cherry Brandy'. Bill arrived home in his usual Saturday night jovial state. Molly arrived soon after. Dinner was uneventful. After dinner, cards. That was the first 'mishap'. Bill insisted on producing and using his 'special' deck and they were striking. Each one had a very attractive young female in various stages of undress and in various provocative poses. One of the more diplomatic boarders eventually convinced him that, with ladies present, they weren't quite appropriate. The usual deck was produced but not before Mum was absolutely mortified.

Then Bill disappeared to his room briefly and reappeared with a ceramic flask of cherry brandy. The distinguishing feature of the flask was the handle—a very nubile girl, very naked, in a very erotically suggestive pose. The contents were offered around the table and, predictably, there were only two takers, Bill and Molly. They proceeded to make a very obvious hole in the contents with many intimate caresses of the handle. Bill and Molly were soon pie-faced and that was when the evening really became interesting as their restraint and baser instincts were loosed on an unsuspecting household.

As the situation became more embarrassing for the adults but more sniggery-hilarious to the less mature, their behaviour became more outrageous. Molly perched herself on Bill's lap. Bill nibbled her ear and throat. Fortunately, his hands were concealed under the table. I think he had a lecture on appropriate and inappropriate behaviour the next day. He appeared quite chastened for a while afterwards. Molly was never invited to dine again. However, she wasn't ostracised completely, not even when she rang us at 3 o'clock one morning. 'Oh, that's why it's so dark,' she muttered when her mistake was pointed out to her.

Molly bought a dog, a lovely little kelpie. When it was realised that dogs like that need exercise, I was willingly co-opted into walking it regularly. I took him for his walk one Sunday and went next door to return the leash as I always did on our return. No matter how hard I knocked on the door there was no answer. Just as I decided she probably had had a hard night and was about to give up, I noticed smoke oozing underneath the door and around the door edges. While I called the fire brigade, Dad forced his way in and slithered on his belly into the kitchen which seemed to be the source of the smoke.

Sure enough, Molly had put a leg of lamb in the oven and gone back to bed. She was out like a light. Molly's only concern when she was roused was the whereabouts of her cat. It was found curled up on a pile of clothes in a wardrobe. The house, and Molly, quickly returned to normal once all of the windows were opened.

Then poor old Molly returned home with a bloke in the cab. He stayed and stayed and stayed and was still there when we moved on. Soon after, the fights started. No violence (I think), but the language certainly extended my vocabulary. I think he was living on whatever income Molly had. We never saw either of them out of the house, except going to or from a cab. But we sure heard them!

I think that I resented the boarding house life sometimes, because of its interference with family life. On looking back I think that I learned a lot about people from various backgrounds and how to communicate with them. I also came to appreciate Mum's attitude that everyone has desirable and undesirable attributes. For these reasons I can say that I had a privileged childhood.

STORIES FROM THE SHED

Darryl Dymock

DARRYL DYMOCK GREW UP in Brisbane but, after initial employment in Queensland, lived much of his working life elsewhere—Port Moresby, Armidale NSW, and Adelaide. He and his wife Cheryl returned to Brisbane in 2005. They have four children and seven grandchildren. Darryl was a National Serviceman 1969–70, and has spent most of his working life in education. Currently he works as a casual lecturer and contracted researcher at Griffith University. He has had five non-fiction books and several short fiction stories published, and is convenor of the writing group at Oxley Men's Shed.

'a' IS LIKE AN APPLE ON A TWIG

Back in 2008 I had phone call from a woman organising a 50-year-reunion for my class at Coorparoo Primary School. I vaguely recognised her name but I'd had no contact with any of my fellow students since I'd left, so I thought it'd be interesting to see where they'd all ended up. I was staggered and disappointed, however, to discover that no one at the reunion actually remembered my being at the school. When I told them my name, they looked at me blankly. The person who'd organised the event had apparently found my name on a list and tracked me down from that.

It was only when the reunion group pinned up a large photo of the class way back that the penny dropped: the photo was of the

Grade 8 class, taken in 1958; I'd only gone to Coorparoo Primary until Grade 6, 1956. It seemed that in those two years they'd managed to forget me! Which shows the sort of impression I'd made in my six years there.

Nevertheless, whatever my classmates' recollections of those years, I have strong if selective memories of my time at Coorparoo State School, a two-storey dark brick edifice at the corner of Cavendish Road and Old Cleveland Road at Coorparoo Junction. My first year, 1951, when I turned six, was spent under the forbidding eye of squat, bespectacled Miss Bligh, who taught us the alphabet: ' 'a' is like an apple on a twig, 'a' says..., 'b' like a bat and ball, 'b' says... , 'c' like a cake with a bite taken out...', etc., and how to write those letters on our slates using special pencils. Copy-books with ruled lines and steel-nibbed pens dipped in ink wells on our desks came later. Sometime during primary school we also made craft objects using matchboxes and wallpaper off-cuts and wool and such, but my teachers were never impressed with my creative efforts, which I realise now must have been ahead of their time.

The whole school had an assembly every morning, and we marched to our classrooms to the tune of *Colonel Bogey*, played over the PA system. Mr Bracewell taught us in Grade 5, distinguished by having only one arm, and we assumed he'd lost the other in World War II, which had finished the year I was born. Our Grade 6 teacher, Mr Smith, was also possibly a war veteran, and was reputed to have a glass eye. Two of the other boys tried to check this out one day by waving a red handkerchief on one side of the alleged false eye to see if Mr Smith would turn towards it. But the result was inconclusive, and the test too potentially dangerous to be repeated.

Punishment for such tomfoolery was typically the 'cuts'—a bamboo cane brought down hard by the teacher or headmaster on the student's outstretched hand, up to six times, depending on the severity of the 'crime'. I was never outgoing enough to be a troublemaker, and, although I remember I had the cane at least once in primary school, I don't recall the misdemeanour.

I did modestly well at primary school, but didn't have any academic highlights. I did manage to be consistently selected for various school rugby league teams. They were in weight divisions—4 stone 7 pounds and 5 stone 10 pounds, and open, I think. The pre-season weigh-in could be an anxious time, and nervous boys often stripped to their jocks to step on the very public scales. I was stocky with no great speed, so inevitably played in the second row of the scrum. On sports afternoons we had to make our own way to footy grounds all over the southside of Brisbane by tram, which was great freedom. The most-feared venue was Davies Park at West End, because some of the opposition were particularly solid and indulged in what we called 'dirty' play, and sometimes had vociferous mothers who waved their black umbrellas at us.

According to Google, Coorparoo State School is two kilometres and 25 minutes' walk from where our family lived, but at the time it seemed a lot longer. On one occasion when I was walking to school with my sister, Heather, who was two years older than me, she suggested we split up and walk around two different sides of a block and meet up on the other side. When I arrived at the end of the block, Heather was nowhere to be seen, and I had no idea where I was. After a while, my tears drew the sympathy of a local resident who took me to school in their car. In fact, however, we three children rarely walked—we either got a lift with the father of a boy who lived around the corner in Orion Street, Mark Smith, in his Dad's Austin A40, or walked up Beresford Terrace and caught the tram that ran down to Coorparoo Junction. In 1955, when I was 10, the trams were replaced by trolley buses, with twin poles projecting from their roof to link up with parallel overhead wires.

One of the benefits of my being pretty well behaved at primary school and doing okay in my studies was being appointed 'milk monitor' in Grade 6. Under a Commonwealth Government nutrition scheme, every child was entitled to a third-pint bottle of milk a day. Vendors unloaded crates of the stuff every morning, and another student and I would deliver a crate of milk to each room before the morning tea break ('little lunch'). This was a great lurk, because not only did it get us out of whatever work the rest of the class was doing, we could have a couple more bottles each if there was any milk left over. Mind you, it was best to down it as soon as possible after delivery because the milk wasn't refrigerated, and the warm Queensland sun quickly took its toll. Some kids even brought flavouring to school to put in the milk to overcome any sour taste. Imagine that, flavoured milk!

The reason I left Coorparoo State School at the end of Grade 6 was because the Department of Public Instruction (as Education Queensland was then called) had recently opened Cavendish Road High and Intermediate School at Holland Park, 1.4 kilometres and 20 minutes' walk from our home. My sister had already made the move, and with some reluctance I agreed to change schools to Cav Road for years 7 and 8 ('Intermediate'). That also meant I could transition more smoothly into the four years of high school hopefully after completing the Scholarship Exam.

I don't think I made any greater mark on my new school in the six years I subsequently spent there, nor did I ever think I would be the sort of kid who skipped classes to play pool or ride the streets in school time on a mate's bicycle. Looking back, I wonder if I ever worked out at the time what school was about, or where I fitted in, despite the best efforts of some dedicated teachers. It took me a few years to reach a point where I genuinely applied myself to study and find what I was capable of.

BEETLEMANIA

It took me a couple of attempts to get my driver's licence. The first time, I backed into a post on the footpath while trying to reverse park. When the testing officer did finally agree I could be unleashed on the streets, it took me a couple more years to save enough to buy a second-hand car.

I was fortunate that my sister's boyfriend was an apprentice mechanic at a car dealer at nearby Stones Corner. One night he turned up at our house at Coorparoo with a VW Beetle he thought might suit me. It was a classic 1960 two-door model in khaki green, with four-on-the-floor gears and 'flipper' indicators instead of flasher lights, but distinguished by having twin copper exhaust pipes the previous owner had fitted. I took the car around the block to pretend I was giving it a test drive but, as a 20 year-old, I was so excited about the prospect of owning my first car that I knew I was going to buy it.

As with all Beetles, the motor was in the back, the fuel tank at the front, and the battery under the back seat. The 1960 version didn't have a fuel gauge, so I had to wait for the engine to splutter to tell me the petrol was low. There was a reserve tank lever on the front firewall next to the pedals, so whenever I heard the ominous gurgle I had to quickly kick the lever from vertical to horizontal and petrol would begin flowing from the reserve tank. That would give me another gallon of gas to make sure I could reach a service station (at least in the city!) In those days, I was too broke to be able to fill the tank, and sometimes I bought only $2 worth of petrol at the bowser.

One evening I was driving my Beetle along Wynnum Road towards East Brisbane beside one of the trams that then ran on that route. The light was fading and there was hardly any traffic. As we came to a sharp right-hand bend in the road, I suddenly realised that there was not enough room for my car and the tram to go around together, so I dropped back. Too late! As the tram turned, the back of it neatly caught the VW's front wraparound bumper bar on the driver's side and yanked it straight off its bolts. The metal bumper bar fell onto the road in front of the car with a loud clatter as I braked to a halt. I watched the lights of the tram recede into the distance, then climbed out of the car, picked up the bumper bar and tossed it on to the back seat. As I drove away I shook my head, stunned by what had just occurred and not quite believing it, as if it had happened in a dream.

On another occasion, I was driving the VW home from my job in the city and had just crossed what is now the William Jolly Bridge into South Brisbane when I smelled something burning. When I looked in the rear vison mirror I saw that the back of the car was filling with smoke. I quickly pulled to the side of the road, jumped out and yanked the front seat forward. The smoke was pouring from under the vinyl-covered back seat and when I pulled it out I could see the kapok stuffing underneath the seat was alight.

Later I found what had happened: Over time the thin asbestos sheet that insulated the metal cover plate from the battery terminals had eroded away, the battery had briefly shorted out and a spark had set fire to the dry stuffing under the seat.

I threw the seat upside down on the footpath and yelled 'Fire!' An old guy came trotting out from a nearby guest house. 'Quick, get some water,' I shouted, and he scurried off. I was still in my long-sleeved white work shirt and tie, and was so desperate that I ripped the shirt off and began beating at the flickering flames.

The guy from the guest house reappeared, carrying a bucket of water. 'Here you go, mate,' he called. As he headed towards me, I could see water spurting from all sides of the old metal container. The bucket had so many holes in it that by the time he reached me it was almost empty. But I threw the last dregs on the now smouldering car seat and between us we managed to put the fire out.

As I stood there gasping from the effort and the surprise, I looked down and saw that I was still wearing my tie; my collar was still around my neck. In my haste, I'd literally ripped the shirt off my body, leaving my collar and tie.

Fortunately there was no serious damage to the car, and I drove it for a couple more years before trading it in on another second-hand VW Beetle. However, as you will see in the next story, a change in circumstances meant I didn't own that second car for long.

A GOLDEN THREAD

My girlfriend Cheryl Ascott lived with her parents in a high-set white weatherboard house with an iron roof in the Brisbane suburb of Holland Park. To look at, there was nothing special about the house, but one summer afternoon something happened there that helped shape how I would spend much of the rest of my life.

It was late 1966, and I'd met Cheryl a year earlier, just after she'd finished high school. In the twelve months we'd known each other, she'd been full-time at the University of Queensland, doing an Arts degree, although her high school marks had been good enough to get her into medicine.

I, on the other hand, had scraped through high school and, by this time, had completed four years as a clerk in the Commonwealth Public Service in the Brisbane CBD. It was a comfortable job, and I liked the people I worked with, but it didn't extend me. So I enrolled in evening classes at university, hoping that might open up some opportunities. But I had no great aspirations.

My two main achievements in those four years after I left school were to save enough money to buy a second-hand VW Beetle and to be selected in the Queensland Junior Rugby Union team. And I had a good-looking girlfriend who was very smart.

When I walked into the lino-floored kitchen at Cheryl's parents' house in Holland Park that November afternoon, her mother Tess immediately said, 'Like a cup of tea?' I'd discovered early in our relationship that the Ascotts liked to drink tea, and I reckoned if I was going to get in good with them, I'd better join in the ritual. So of course I said, 'Yes, please, Mrs Ascott. That'd be great.'

The hot topic of conversation that afternoon was Cheryl's decision to drop out of university and go to teachers' college instead. Despite predictably excellent grades, she hadn't been rapt with her first year of university life, and reckoned that teaching held more appeal than the career in the foreign service a vocational counsellor had suggested.

At that time, Queensland was desperately short of teachers, and Cheryl had been accepted into a fast-track program for high school teaching. All she needed was to have completed one year of university with relevant studies, and then undertake a one-year teacher training course at Kelvin Grove Teachers College. This would be followed by a post-training year teaching in a school. Trainee teachers would be paid an allowance for the year they were at college.

Cheryl's older brother, Frank, had gone to uni, but her two older sisters had left school at the end of junior high school, so I think her parents were a bit surprised she didn't want to take more advantage of the opportunity. But they supported her decision to go to teacher's college, particularly as Frank had recently become a teacher after completing a degree and graduate diploma.

That afternoon, Cheryl's father Maurie was out on his rounds, dropping off bundles of newspapers for the newsagents' and sidewalk sellers' afternoon sales. As the three of us chatted around the kitchen table about Cheryl's forthcoming transition, I said, 'I can't imagine doing that. I don't think I'd make a very good teacher.'

I thought I was a pretty conscientious clerk, and I didn't mind the hurly burly of rugby, but I just couldn't imagine myself standing in front of a blackboard and trying to teach a class of teenagers, and certainly not a bunch of primary school ankle-biters.

Tess Ascott put down her cup carefully into its saucer. 'I think you'd make a good teacher,' she said.

I looked at her incredulously. 'Do you? I've never seriously thought about it.' There was no history of teachers in the Dymock family—my father's family came from farming stock and he himself was a concreter. My maternal grandfather did something in a city office in the railways.

'Well, perhaps you should think about it,' my future mother-in-law said.

Cheryl immediately picked up on the idea. 'Why don't you come to teachers college with me next year?' she said. 'You've got the equivalent of a year's university study from your evening courses, so you'd be eligible.' She kindly didn't add that, as with high school, I'd scraped through those four subjects. It depended on how desperate the Queensland Education Department was for high school teachers.

Driving home to Coorparoo afterwards, I went back over the discussion in my mind. Me, a teacher? Could Cheryl's mother be right? After four years in the public service, was this the opportunity I'd been looking for? I knew I was capable of more than I was doing. But teaching?

In the morning, I knew I could do it if I wanted to. And I'd get to go to teacher's college with my girlfriend. I put in my application (late) and waited. I imagined my name was very near the bottom of the priority list, and that the selectors were hoping someone with better qualifications might come along. Christmas came and went, then January, and I still hadn't heard anything. It looked like I was going to miss out.

Then, bang! With one week to go before the college term started, I received a letter of acceptance. The Education Department really was desperate! I felt bad because I had to give very short notice at my workplace, where the bosses and my colleagues had been good to me. What's more, I had to sell my VW because on my trainee teacher allowance I couldn't afford the repayments. I replaced it with a fully-paid-for oil-burning Simca that Cheryl sometimes had to push to get started (but she still married me later anyway).

My future mother-in-law couldn't have foreseen what effect her encouragement would have on my career and future life. I graduated from teachers' college at the end of 1967, and spent the next year teaching at Herberton Secondary Department ('high top') in North Queensland. At the end of that year, Cheryl and I were married, six weeks before I was conscripted into the Army for two years. Because I was a teacher, after basic training I was fortunate to be selected for the Educational Corps and posted to Papua New Guinea (PNG) for 12 months to teach troops of the Pacific Islands Regiment, instead of to the precarious fighting front in Vietnam, as many of my fellow conscripts were. I quickly learned that I was a better teacher of adults than teenagers, a discovery that I'm sure rescued me and a generation of high schoolers from some potentially miserable years. As a result of my time in PNG, two years after my discharge from the Army I returned to Port Moresby with my family for another three years, teaching upcoming public servants at what was then called the Administrative College. That experience with teaching adults, many of whom lived in residential colleges on campus, led to appointments at the University of New England, Armidale, where I completed my Masters degree and then a PhD in Education, and where we lived for 25 years while we brought up our four children. Those were stimulating and sometimes challenging years in a variety of educational settings, including a short job exchange in England.

Subsequently, I had a senior education appointment for three years in a government agency in Adelaide, after which I retired from full-time paid employment. I've spent the years since our return to Brisbane in 2005 in satisfying part-time roles at Griffith University, teaching, researching and publishing with a small team in the School of Education and Professional Studies, work that continues to this day. It's a continuation of a golden thread that started more than 50 years ago that afternoon in my (late) mother-in-law's kitchen. It taught me that sometimes we need other people to recognise our strengths.

www.ingramcontent.com/pod-product-compliance
Lightning Source LLC
Chambersburg PA
CBHW071526080526
44588CB00011B/1572